FICTIONS OF BUSINESS

*Insights on Management
from Great Literature*

Robert A. Brawer

JOHN WILEY & SONS, INC.

New York ◆ Chichester ◆ Weinheim ◆ Brisbane
Singapore ◆ Toronto

ISBN 0-471-17999-X

For Catherine
In world nis non so wyter mon
That al hire bounte telle con

CONTENTS

Success in today's consumer-driven world requires, above all, a sense of theater. Entrepreneurs' ability to conjure up images and illusions that confer a unique value on their goods and services is their key to success in a saturated global market. This chapter discusses two works of fiction that offer a fresh perspective on how successful salespeople can convince us to buy what we may not need—or even want: Theodore Dreiser's *Sister Carrie* and David Mamet's *Glengarry Glen Ross*.

The truly "self-made man" of Horatio Alger fame often does not conform to the rags-to-riches stereotype. Instead, many "self-made" businesspeople merely create for themselves an image, or an illusion of success, that generates positive perceptions from society. This chapter com-

pares the real world with the fictional by discussing
Horatio Alger's *Ragged Dick* as well as two other works of
fiction whose characters have succeeded solely on their
self-made images: Geoffrey Chaucer's *The Canterbury
Tales* and Anthony Trollope's *The Way We Live Now*.

The fear of losing our individuality and becoming just a
cog in the corporate wheel is part of American business
mythology. This chapter discusses three works of fiction
that demonstrate how self-awareness is the key to being a
self-empowered manager and, alternately, how the failure
to be honest with ourselves can be personally and professionally disabling: Sloan Wilson's *The Man in the Grey
Flannel Suit*, Arthur Miller's *Death of a Salesman*, and
John P. Marquand's *Point of No Return*.

The predisposition to believe what we want to believe
and to screen out what runs counter to our interests and
biases is endemic to corporate life: Managers often tend
to reinforce one another's opinions and to expedite action plans rather than to scrutinize the data and assumptions that underlie them. This chapter discusses two
works of fiction that show us how vulnerable we are to
the will to believe and how self-defeating it can be to ad-
here to corporate gospel: Joseph Heller's *Something Happened* and George Bernard Shaw's *Major Barbara*.

5. Survival of the Fittest in a Darwinian Business World   139

"Survival of the fittest" characterizes much of business today. Self-interest and efficiency are critical to success, but not at the expense of ethical responsibility and compassion toward the people we manage and the customers we serve. This chapter discusses five works of fiction that can help us assess our corporate values and responsibility to the larger community: Theodore Dreiser's *The Financier*, Sinclair Lewis's *Babbitt*, John Dos Passos's *The Big Money*, Upton Sinclair's *The Jungle*, and Mark Twain's *A Connecticut Yankee in King Arthur's Court*.

6. Office Politics, Stress Management, and Chaos   185

Dealing with personality conflicts and office politics is sometimes a manager's most demanding, infuriating, and time-consuming responsibility. It therefore requires the utmost ingenuity and resourcefulness. This chapter discusses three works of fiction that illustrate how some managers deal effectively—and some not so effectively—with people fighting for power (sometimes literally): Wilfred Sheed's *Office Politics*, James Thurber's "The Catbird Seat," and Joseph Conrad's "Typhoon."

Conclusion: The More Things Change . . .   221

Notes   225

INTRODUCTION:
THE FICTIONS OF BUSINESS
AND THE BUSINESS
OF FICTION

The most complex and persistent problems facing us as managers and executives in corporate life are often distinctively human problems. How do we maintain our individuality in adapting to the corporate culture? How do we maintain our personal integrity when corporate gospel compels unquestioned assent? How can we reconcile what we owe ourselves as individuals with our responsibilities to the companies we represent? How can we manage interpersonal conflicts without disrupting the organization? How can we keep our perspectives in a consumer-driven society in which everyone is vulnerable to the selling of image and illusion? How can we balance self-interest and efficiency with humane values in a world where only the fittest survive? These and related issues are recurrent; they compel our attention, and they call less on our professional expertise than on our personal resources and judgment.

I have always felt that imaginative literature is an invaluable but untapped resource for executives trying to understand and resolve perennial human problems in business. I say *human* problems advisedly. Novels and plays about corporate life are impractical in that they provide no guidance about the intricacies of production control, demographics, information systems, or accounting. They do help us, though, to understand our basic needs and those of the people we manage: the need for identity, for self-esteem, for power, for control, for mental challenge, for acceptance, for security, for self-fulfillment, and for recognition.

Imaginative writers demonstrate how these fundamental motives which also drive us as individuals affect our attitudes, behaviors, and decisions as executives. In addition, they show us what the consequences of our actions will likely be. The hindsight that writers give us is a real advantage, since we are so often unable to see beyond the immediate moment or situation; and we often have trouble resolving distinctively human issues in the workplace with finality.

Immersion in the world of imaginative writing clearly has nothing directly to do with maintaining a respectable bottom line, controlling inventory levels, or drafting a marketing plan. I would insist, however, that the values and insights we glean from serious literature sensitize us to ourselves and, by extension, to the problems inherent in managing people in an organization. I mean to cite chapter and verse, quite literally, in showing that intelligent managers can profit at least as much from reading distinguished novelists and playwrights who have taken businesspeople and our business-oriented culture as a literary subject, as they can, for instance, from reading any number of management handbooks offering easy-to-fathom panaceas for beleaguered companies.

Who *are* the people who populate the enduring novels and plays about life in business? Memorable people, to be sure. Among them is an astute arms manufacturer who disdains the poor and all forms of charity. Another is an ingratiating real estate salesman adept at convincing people to invest their life savings in property they will never see. Yet another is an imposing tycoon who, in a dog-eat-dog world, rides roughshod over conventional morality in his lust for wealth and power. I have deliberately singled out individuals whom we might ordinarily shun. Yet they possess qualities that command our attention as managers and executives: an indestructible belief in themselves combined with an equally solid sense of what it takes to succeed in the real world.

I feel as if I know each of these people intimately. Strictly speaking, they are no more than figments of the imagination. A writer's imagination. Yet George Bernard Shaw's industrialist, Andrew Undershaft; David Mamet's salesman, Richard Roma; and Theodore Dreiser's financier, Frank Cowperwood, engage us as businesspeople and as individuals because what they are made to say and do reflects what we can imagine ourselves saying and doing under generally similar circumstances. Whenever I think about these characters, the artificial boundaries we erect between fact and fiction, the real world and the world of the imagination, quickly dissolve.

The claims I make for applying the insights gained from fiction to the realities of the workplace derive mainly from my own double orientation, first as a faculty member of a

university English department and, later, as an executive
and CEO of Maidenform, Inc., an internationally recognized women's apparel firm. Few can appreciate, as I do, the
mental gulf that exists between professions so dissimilar in
character and aim. Over my 20-year life as an executive, I
was constantly asked by business associates how it felt being
in the "real" world. The answer I gave was surprising and
even puzzling to many people. I said I wasn't sure I was currently in the "real" world, since my present job as a marketer
of a venerable American brand—creating and sustaining
"brand equity"—dealt as much with perception as with
actuality. Brand equity is the sum total of all the perceptions
consumers have about a brand and its consequent value for
them. Long-term profitable growth, a real enough goal for
management, depends on capturing the minds of consumers, so that they will buy your product, even at a pre-
mium, rather than another brand offering similar functional
benefits. My own objective as a marketing executive was to
generate, primarily through national consumer advertising,
positive perceptions of our brand as the brand of choice.

Now without being philosophical, you could argue that
the perception *is* the reality. I would insist only that the
profession of teaching English has as legitimate a claim to
reality as does the world of business. It is just as vital for
good teachers to engage the minds of their students as it is
for professional marketers to capture the minds of their target audiences.

Our tendency to compartmentalize our professions and
disciplines is widespread. Work and leisure, the life of the
mind and the practical life, the humanities and commerce,
writers and businesspeople, seem mutually exclusive. Yet the

distinctions we commonly draw between the world of commerce and the world of the imagination have little historical or theoretical basis. Geoffrey Chaucer, the fourteenth-century author of *The Canterbury Tales*, spent more of his time as a controller of customs and royal building projects than as a poet reciting his stories on demand at the court of Richard II. Similarly, the author of *The Merchant of Venice* was a shrewd businessman who came by his knowledge of contracts, finance, and business risk in the process of handling his own affairs. In fact, until the mid-nineteenth century in America, merchants thought of themselves and were generally regarded as men of intellect and culture. Indeed, a humanistic education was regarded as a distinct advantage in commercial enterprises.

For me, the genius of George Bernard Shaw lies in his ability to puncture the stereotypes we find so comfortable and comforting to create. The munitions manufacturer, Andrew Undershaft, and his daughter's fiancé, a pedantic professor of Greek, appear to be natural adversaries in *Major Barbara*— that is, until we are made to realize how self-serving the professor is and, to the contrary, how Undershaft, the capitalist, embodies the virtues of a humanistic culture.

The fictions of business are indispensable to us because it is the business of fiction to recreate the world we know, or think we know, to make us see it—and ourselves—with new eyes. The examples I select to illustrate some of the universal human issues in business range across the centuries. In the kinds of insights they offer, though, they are equally current. Why? Because they do *not* traffic in the fashionable buzzwords and managerial ideologies of the day, but rather stimulate reflection on the motives, ideas, and principles that govern human affairs, regardless of time, place, and circumstances.

By its nature, this book is a hybrid. It is neither a historical survey of novels and plays about business, nor a history of Maidenform, nor a personal memoir of my career with the company until my retirement in 1995. Rather, it is a series of essays intended to offer fresh perspectives on familiar business problems through a synthesis of these elements. I mix in more or less equal parts my experiences as an insatiable reader and teacher of serious fiction and as an executive engaged with the kinds of issues that typically require creativity and imagination for their resolution. If there is an overall theme that emerges from this witches' brew, it is that the distinctions between art and life, the real world and the world of fiction, are far too slight to be significant.

The six chapters that follow explore human issues that have engaged me constantly over the course of my working life. Chapter One, "Selling as Theater: The Art of Dazzling the Customer," highlights the importance of image and illusion in American business life and, at the same time, our own vulnerability to purveyors of illusion. Chapter Two, "Selling on a Grand Scale: Playing to an Image-Conscious Society," looks at the effect, for better and worse, of assorted "self-made" individuals on a society driven by commercial values. Chapter Three, "Maintaining Individuality in Corporate Life," emphasizes the need to preserve a sense of your personal identity and integrity while satisfying the requirements of the organization. Chapter Four, "Overcoming Corporate Gospel and the Will to Believe," is about how a company's collective faith in its own doctrine can disable it. Chapter Five, "Survival of the Fittest in a Darwinian Business World," examines the strengths as well as limitations of the values required for adapting to a business environment where only the fittest survive. Chapter Six, "Office Politics, Stress Management, and Chaos," examines both the responsibilities of a leader in containing the interpersonal conflicts that sap the strength of an organization and the various options he or she has in resolving them.

A common complaint on the part of managers nowadays is that they are on information overload, ingesting rather than digesting what comes down to them along the "information highway." On the other hand, reading fiction, while also time-consuming, is interactive. We cannot help but reflect on both the relationship between fictional characters and the dilemmas they face and our own experiences and observations of the contemporary business world. Each chapter, therefore, interweaves fictional business situations and characters with their real-life counterparts. I do not expect this double perspective to yield automatic resolutions to the issues I have raised here. Rather, I intend wherever possible to stimulate reflection on the variety of ways in which we might better understand and deal with these issues. It would be difficult to confer with more eminent consultants for this purpose than English and American writers of the caliber of Geoffrey Chaucer, Anthony Trollope, Joseph Conrad, George Bernard Shaw, Theodore Dreiser, Sinclair Lewis, John Dos Passos, James Thurber, John P. Marquand, Arthur Miller, Joseph Heller, and David Mamet. I might add that a subsidiary aim of this book is to encourage the reading of the works discussed here in their entirety, not only as fiction about life in business, but also for the sheer enjoyment they offer as fiction.

SELLING AS THEATER: THE ART OF DAZZLING THE CUSTOMER

A guy comes up to you. . . . "There're these properties *I'd like for you to see." What does it mean? What you want it to mean.*

David Mamet, *Glengarry Glen Ross*

If I were asked to identify a single characteristic that the best businesspeople have in common, I would say that it is a sense of theater. Like theatrical impresarios, they have mastered the art of illusion: creating the perception in the minds of their customers that the product or service they are selling has a unique value that transcends the usual "features and benefits," and does more than satisfy customer "wants or needs." Like great actors, these businesspeople are as adept at selling themselves as they are their products. Like great playwrights, they know their audience and understand how to make their customers feel good about doing business with them. Indeed, they may even change the way their customers look at *themselves*.

In today's consumer-driven culture, I maintain that this kind of salesmanship—or more accurately, *show*manship—is more than an entrepreneurial virtue. It is a necessity. How many enterprises, after all, depend for their sustained profitability on "impulse purchases," on enticing people to spend money on things they may *not* want or need as much as on those they do? Without a sense of theater, an entrepreneur is hard put to survive in a global market where duplication of product offerings creates seemingly unlimited choice, where so many new products proliferate and so few survive, where shelf space is so scarce and shelf life so short, where established worldwide brands are threatened by cheaper private label imitations.

In fact, American merchants' recognition that great theater and great salesmanship are indissolubly linked spans the entire twentieth century. The department store retailers whose stores have survived the century were pioneers in theatrical display. From lavish window displays and opulent decor to counter fixtures and costumed mannequins, merchant-impresarios like Marshall Field, John Wanamaker, and R. H. Macy made the shopping experience a kind of fantasy fulfillment for a mass market. We find this sense of theater articulated even in so unlikely a place as the "Minutes of the Board of Operations" at Macy's in 1902: "The selling departments is [sic] the stage upon which the play is enacted."[1]

In his 1900 novel, *Sister Carrie*, Theodore Dreiser captures the blandishments of a consumer culture most vividly. At the beginning of the novel, Carrie Meeber, a poor farm girl from Wisconsin recently arrived in Chicago, is dazzled by the display of goods in a department store where she has gone to seek work as a clerk:

> [The department stores] were handsome, bustling, suc-
> cessful affairs, with a host of clerks and a swarm of patrons.
> Carrie passed along the busy aisles, much affected by the
> remarkable displays of trinkets, dress goods, stationery,
> and jewelry. Each separate counter was a show place of
> dazzling interest and attraction. She could not help feel-
> ing the claim of each trinket and valuable upon her per-
> sonally, and yet she did not stop. There was nothing there
> which she could not have used—nothing which she did
> not long to own. The dainty slippers and stockings, the
> delicately frilled skirts and petticoats, the laces, ribbons,
> haircombs, purses, all touched her with individual desire,
> and she felt keenly the fact that not any of these things
> were in the range of her purchase.[2]

The desire that Dreiser's Carrie feels here is not simply the longing of a lonely young woman in the big city for the first time. It is an enduring characteristic of American con-sumers in a land of plenty. So, too, is the ingenuity with which American retailers continue to fabricate ever more theatrical scenarios to feed the public's apparently insatiable appetite for shopping—or, as promoters say nowadays, for a shopping *experience*.

There is a clear trajectory from Marshall Field's first showcase window to the recently unveiled theme mall in Las Vegas, "unlike anything the retail world has ever seen," according to a recent *Wall Street Journal* report.[3] A 50-foot

Trojan horse "that rocks, snorts steam and shoots lasers"; an hourly recreation of the sinking of Atlantis "in a riot of steam, fire, and water"; a chariot race à la Ben Hur that takes place five times a day "as diners and shoppers look on"; and singing gondoliers poling shoppers along an indoor canal are some of the features driving retail sales in this mall-to-end-all-malls. Selling as theater has here reached its apogee—at least for the present. Sales are reported to be at an all-time high.

The businesspeople with a sense of theater know that there is a basic psychology in play here. They know that most people are predisposed to buy, and they know how to tap into that predisposition through theatrical-style illusion. Illusion makes reality, or what we might call the *everydayness* of things, palatable. The fabricating of illusion, therefore, has always been intrinsic to the art of selling goods and services. In our time, selling as theater is no different in principle from what it was in 1900. It is simply being raised to a higher power.

I propose two relatively unfamiliar ways to collect some very specific and, I think, useful data about consumer purchasing behavior, and about how businesspeople conjure up unique perceptions of their products and themselves to drive sales in oversaturated markets. First, by defying conventional market-research wisdom and looking at your own mind-set and characteristics as a consumer, you can pretty much divine how others will react to the same stimuli. Though we like to *think* of ourselves as unique, we are not; our behavior as consumers is remarkably consistent in certain ways with that of millions of others in our consumer-driven culture—differences in background, spending power, and personalities notwithstanding. Second, I am convinced that a reading of some of the fictions of business, precisely because they are *imaginative* in nature, can give us a range of fresh perspectives on what the fine art of selling as theater has always been about.

To begin with, then, two simple examples from my own history as a consumer.

T-Shirts and Other Fictions

I recently bought three T-shirts from *The J. Peterman Company Owner's Manual* that I didn't need and don't wear. If I had seen them on display in a store, I would doubtless have passed them up. Their heavy cotton fabric is uncomfortable, and their dull grey and brown colors are unattractive. Yet I gladly bought them for more money than I normally spend on shirts that I *do* wear.

The truth is that I love reading the Peterman catalogues and look forward to each new one in the same way as I do the latest novel by John Le Carré. For the Peterman catalogue reads like great escapist fiction. A sketch of a very ordinary blue blazer appears under the rubric *British Unflappability* (*The Niven Blazer*), with this description:

> Some men can emerge from a smoking bomb crater
>   looking incredibly relaxed, even elegant.
> Are they born that way?
> Some actually are.
> Others are just lucky enough to be wearing a navy blue
>   blazer at the time. . . .

Blazers give you the gift of looking *right* . . . But you
already knew that. In fact you probably already own
one or two. Why, then, this Blazer?
Because this is the blazer of Niven and Grant. Of O'Toole
and Howard and Bond. It is: classic, chic, cocky,
comfortable, casual, cool, charismatic, clean-lined,
and altogether unflappable.

J. Peterman has done his homework. He knows very well
that I already have a blue blazer, but not quite the kind that
will put me in company with these suave gents, including
Howard (Leslie, of course). A *Niven* blazer, on the other
hand, will time-warp me in the romance of a bygone era and
transform me into a living legend. Look, even the details—
"slightly suppressed waist," "flapped patch pockets," "3¾
inch lapels"—proclaim it's me. Why, J. Peterman has said as
much: "Is that you in the mirror? It is."

Even a simple T-shirt takes on magical properties under
this format. Who could care about fit or comfort or contemporary styling when you are wearing the very shirt Persian
princes wore for battle-training in the fifteenth century?
The illuminated manuscript from 1472 that J. Peterman has
unearthed in the British Museum actually shows a horseman
wearing one of the six "seriously faded vintage colors" the
T-shirt comes in. Holding back a little, I limit myself to
three.

Sure, I admit to sharing the irritation of friends hooked
on J. Peterman when what arrives in the mail somehow
doesn't match what we could have sworn the catalogue
described. There it is, just a dumb T-shirt. But that's OK.
I've had my fix.

What do I conclude from all this? Someone at J. Peterman has mastered the indispensable art of creating a demand precisely for what their customers do *not* want or need. Run-of-the-mill salespeople have always insisted that everything begins with product. Whenever I hear that tired axiom, I cringe. In a society awash in consumer products, one interchangeable with another, the product is secondary. It is the *fiction* that counts.

Most of us, if pressed, will own up to being vulnerable to J. Peterman-type appeals. The unworn T-shirts will not, I am certain, be my last purchase from this catalogue. Actually, the cost of reveling in illusions like this seems worth it, especially when we can suspend our better judgment with impunity.

Here is a related example of how to create the perception of added value in the mind of the consumer. Some years ago, my wife and I bought a piece of Chinese export porcelain to add to our modest collection. It was a small blue and white saucer very much like thousands of other examples that figured in the eighteenth-century trade between Europe and China. The dealer, an acquaintance of mine from whom we had bought several other pieces of Chinese export porcelain, explained that *this* saucer was special, because it had been retrieved from the Geldermalsen, a Dutch ship that sank in 1752 with a full cargo of wares en route from China to Holland. He showed us a glossy, lavishly illustrated book that gave the history of the ship, together with photographs of the pieces that had been dredged up, many identical to the saucer in his hand. Not only was the familiar blue glaze badly faded, but several barnacles still clung to the rim of the saucer. The price? Just double what we had paid the same dealer for a similar piece only a few months earlier. His explanation was simple—and, I must confess, persuasive: "You're buying a little piece of history."

The Geldermalsen special sits on our mantle, barnacles intact, a faded example of export porcelain, but an authentic reminder of the perils the old Dutch sea captains encountered in the China Sea.

There are moments when I cannot help wondering how much more intrinsically valuable (and cheaper) our eighteenth-century piece of history would have been had it *not* lain on the bottom of the sea collecting ocean matter—and its signature barnacles—for over 200 years. But then I reflect, without a trace of irony, on the ability of imaginative entrepreneurs to sell T-shirts and antique porcelain by reorienting consumers as to what it is they are *really* buying or collecting. (Come to think of it, a Geldermalsen T-shirt would have gone nicely with my Geldermalsen book and saucer.)

Of course, these are both harmless examples in the sense that I willingly participated in being set up. In such cases, it is easy for us to laugh at ourselves. It costs us nothing. But what happens if we take this process a step further? Few of us would admit that we can be convinced to act against our own best interests and instincts, especially when it comes to spending real money. Few of us realize, on the other hand, how strong a hold a conjuror of illusion can exert on us under the right conditions. In his play *Glengarry Glen Ross*, the American dramatist David Mamet sets the full power of the salesman as illusionist vividly before us in words and action.

Selling as Theater: *Glengarry Glen Ross*

In 1984 David Mamet received the Pulitzer prize for a drama about what it takes to survive in the dog-eat-dog world of real estate transactions. Glengarry Glen Ross is the name a shady real estate firm invents to glorify a worthless piece of property in Florida that the firm's salesmen will try to sell to unwary buyers. To sell the Glengarry plots, the salesmen all depend on the availability of "leads," or potential customers, in the company's files. To stimulate business, the firm's owners, who never appear on stage, encourage a decidedly *un*friendly competition among the Glengarry salesmen. They give the prime leads to those who bring in the most business and the worst leads to the least successful, who have to make their quotas under these onerous conditions or be fired.

The desperation that arises from this situation fuels the plot of the play. In the first scene we see one of the weaker salesmen struggling to survive by trying to bribe the company's office manager for the most promising leads; and then, in the second scene, two others plotting to rifle through the files of the head office and then sell the company's best leads to a competitor.

Richard Roma is the company's top dog (I use the word advisedly here) because for him *everyone* is a potential client, and he is relentless in giving chase. Mamet shows us his star salesman's stuff in a brief self-contained scene in the middle of the play. There we see Roma engaging a stranger in an adjoining booth of a Chinese restaurant in a casual, apparently aimless conversation. It would actually be more accurate to describe the scene as a monologue that is a tour

de force of salesmanship. Ever the opportunist, Roma
quickly sets up his man to do a deal without the other getting a word or even a thought in edgewise.

It is difficult to capture the flavor of Roma's pitch simply
by paraphrasing it. Mamet wants us to see the salesman
improvising in a chance encounter, so his speech seems
wordy and disjointed. Its operative idea—that we should
not let convention deter us from going after what we
want—is cheap; but the way Roma serves up the idea to his
mark, a man named Lingk, is unique. Before quoting
directly from the play, I should point out that Mamet has
Roma pitch his potential client in gutter language that may
be shocking to the audience, but that has a special dramatic
function in this scene as we shall see:

> . . . all train compartments smell vaguely of shit. It gets
> so you don't mind it. That's the worst thing I can confess.
> You know how long it took me to get there? A long time.
> When you *die* you're going to regret the things you don't
> do. You think you're *queer* . . . ? I'm going to tell you
> something: we're *all* queer. You think that you're a *thief*?
> So *what*? You get befuddled by a middle class
> morality . . . ? Get *shut* of it. Shut it out. You cheated on
> your wife . . . ? You *did* it, *live* with it . . . You fuck little
> girls, so *be* it. Bad people go to hell? I don't *think* so.
> (GGR, 47)[4]

Outrageous? Certainly. Yet, as the playwright well
knows, outrageous people often get away with more than
anyone else. That is especially the case when the lines are

delivered in a casual, throwaway manner (at least that is how Al Pacino does it in the film version). This particular opening serves Roma's purposes well. The obscenities divert his prospect's attention from the salesman's objective—to sell him a piece of Glengarry Glen Ross. At the same time, Roma is suggesting exotic possibilities to this apparently lonely man in the next booth that clearly lie outside his "middle class morality."

This is the strategy that Roma, warming to his subject, pursues in this chance encounter. Arousing the man's prurient instincts, Roma moves him toward what he calls "the moment":

> The great fucks that you may have had. What do you remember about them? . . . For *me*, I'm saying, what it is, it's probably not the orgasm. Some broads, forearms on your neck, something her *eyes* did . . . Eh? What I'm saying, what is our life? It's looking forward and it's looking back. And that's our life. That's *it*. Where is the *moment*? (GGR, 48)

Where, indeed? For most of his monologue, Roma violates some of the most sacred real-life canons of salesmanship. For one thing, he never stops talking; for another, he never stops talking about himself. But that is just the point. Roma must predispose his man to do a deal he would ordinarily run from by getting him to buy into the idea of seizing the day (the "moment"). He can do this only by releasing all the inhibitions, all the built-in restraints that might get in the way. In itself, Roma's philosophy is nickle-and-dime stuff. Life is full of contingencies, Roma says in a barrage of words, so that to be secure under the circumstances, "I do those things which seem correct to me *today*." A perfectly reasonable way to live, this. Who would deny that it is best to be the master of one's fate?

The devil, though, is in the details. This is how Roma's life-affirming philosophy figures in the context of his sales pitch:

> I do those things which seem correct to me *today* . . .
> According to the dictates of my mind . . . Stocks, bonds,
> objects of art, real estate. Now: what are they? . . . An
> opportunity. To what? To make money? Perhaps. To *lose*
> money? Perhaps. To indulge and to learn about ourselves?
> Perhaps. So *fucking what*? What isn't? They're an *opportu-
> nity*. (GGR, 49)

Roma knows that to predispose this individual to a deal that he neither wants nor needs, the salesman must create the illusion in Lingk's mind that he is indeed his own man. By dismissing the idea that nothing in this world can prevent him from doing what will make him secure and self-confident, Roma gives him title, in effect, to his own existence, with unlimited freedom to act on his impulses. In other words, the salesman knows that to pull off his improbable coup, he must change Lingk's own *self-perception*; he must give him a completely new and more attractive *image* of himself than this apparently lonely man is likely to have possessed before. Roma is subtly removing the grounds on which Lingk might reject the deal, so that closing the sale will be a foregone conclusion.

Adroit salesman that he is, Roma is quick to stress the benefits of availing yourself of life's random offerings, whatever form these may take:

> A guy comes up to you . . . "There're these *properties* I'd like for you to see." What does it mean? What you *want* it to mean. (*Pause.*) Money? (*Pause.*) If that's what it signifies to you. Security? (*Pause.*) Comfort? (*Pause.*) All it is is THINGS THAT HAPPEN TO YOU. (*Pause.*) That's all it is. (GGR, 50)

It is not property Roma is selling here so much as himself. It is up to the actor playing Roma to make sure we see the salesman himself as a great actor. (Knowing how to freight a pause with meaning is perhaps more of a test of a good actor and good salesperson than finding the right way to deliver the words.)

The last part of Roma's pitch fuels the illusions he is creating here. Once Lingk buys into what Roma is saying—not that he has any choice in the matter—he will have attained a remarkable sense of his own uniqueness: "What's special . . . what *draws* us? . . . We're all different . . . We're not the same . . . We are not the same." Roma is a master of the obvious. With his new sense of self, Lingk will clearly make the big decision for himself. As the scene ends, Mamet shows his star salesman at his canniest, for Roma appears as uncertain as we might expect his *prospect* to be:

> I want to show you something. (*Pause.*) It might mean *nothing* to you . . . and it might not. I don't know. I don't know anymore. (GGR, 50)

The playwright is careful to have Roma violate the canons of good salesmanship by *not* having him carry on about the features and benefits of what it is he is actually selling. To have done so would have been to blur Mamet's real point—that Roma, a conjurer of illusion, has sold his client—in every sense—a new lease on life.

Playing by the Rules: The "Highly Effective" Real Estate Salesman in Real Life

Of course, playwrights often use dramatic license to compress time, so that what is accomplished on stage takes a much shorter time than it does in real life. In the real world, no salesperson could be expected to pull off what Roma does in the scene's overall playing time of six or seven minutes. I was reminded of the difference between what a playwright can manage in that time and the time such transactions actually take while reading Stephen R. Covey's best-selling book, *The Seven Habits of Highly Effective People.*[5] There the author, a much sought after management consultant, describes a real estate deal that took six months to consummate.

Covey's book, first published in 1989, has proven one of the most popular books among business leaders and executives in our time. It is still high up on the *Times* paperback list of management best-sellers and has been read, endorsed by prominent chief executives of Fortune 500 companies, and ordered in bulk for distribution down the managerial ranks. It is easy to see why. Covey's prescribed habits promise great things. Put into practice, they bespeak self-mastery and leadership capability. How can any can-do executive go wrong by being "proactive" (Habit 1), by putting "first things first" (Habit 3), by thinking "win-win" (Habit 4), and by "syner- gizing" (Habit 6)? Thanks to Covey, these terms have become ingrained in the language of business.

But there is more to *The Seven Habits* than a handy work- ing vocabulary. As executives become more effective at what they do by applying these habits in business transactions, they promise to become better *people* as well. The same holds for nonbusiness types, too. Everyone who has learned to be proactive and to think positively stands to benefit from an "upward spiral of growth" leading ineluctably "to new levels of understanding" and perfection of character. It is this self- actualizing aspect of Covey's book, I think, that has endeared it to such a wide range of people, not just the high-profile executive.

Covey's timing, too, could not have been better. The subtitle of his work, *Restoring the Character Ethic*, showed his understanding that people at the end of the eighties were fed up with the profligacy and chicanery of that high-flying decade. His book was (and remains) a clarion call to those hungry for ways to be highly effective and ethical at the same time.

Integral to Covey's system of self- and professional renewal is his Habit 5: Seek First to Understand, Then to Be Understood. Remarking that "few people have had any training in listening," the author finds that "our conversa- tions become collective monologues, and [that] we never really understand what's going on inside another human being." For Covey, the important thing on a professional as well as personal plane is "empathic listening"—getting "inside another person's frame of reference," so that "you see the world the way they see the world . . . you understand how they feel." Empathic listening is built "on a base of character that inspires openness and trust." To use a favorite Covey metaphor, seeking first to understand helps build the "Emotional Bank Accounts that create a commerce between hearts."

Covey's prime example of this principle from the world of business comes from a real estate agent who, after taking Covey's seminar in empathic listening, closed an important deal. As this individual relates his experience to Covey, he had been working on the deal for over six months. ". . . all my eggs were in this one basket. All of them." As he went to close the deal at long last, the principals in the transaction, accompanied by their attorneys, brought another real estate agent in "with an alternative proposal" to the very one they had come to sign.

As Covey's real estate agent remembers it, the deal seemed about to fall through until, resolving to "practice what [he] learned" in the Covey seminar he had just attended, he sought to understand the principals' "needs and concerns." In the middle of this phase of the discussion, one of the principals suddenly got up, phoned his wife, put his hand over the mouthpiece, and said to Covey's real estate agent, "You've got the deal." The agent confessed to being "totally dumbfounded" at having managed to con-clude the transaction.

According to Covey, his real estate agent "had made a huge deposit in the Emotional Bank Account" by giving the individuals with whom he was trying to close the deal "psy-chological air." Perhaps so. We would like to think that all such crises can be resolved by recourse to the principle of "empathic communication."

Just suppose, however, that we had come across this story apart from its context in *The Seven Habits*. What then? Would we see it as an example of how we will meet with unexpected success if only we seek "to understand"? I don't think so. Without altering the external facts of the story as Covey retells it, I see the real estate agent and his newly won deal-making prowess in a less flattering light than Covey, his seminar leader, does. Here is my unfiltered version of the incident:

The last-minute ploy of bringing an alternative real estate agent in at the eleventh hour was clearly meant to intimidate Covey's agent and put the squeeze on him for more advantageous terms. The other side's timing was exquisite: Because the agent, as they doubtless knew, had all his "eggs in one basket," he might readily give in on some crucial points. Besides, he would hardly want to abandon the deal after working on it for half a year. They succeeded in convincing Covey's beleaguered agent that he was about to lose the deal. By his own account, he "panicked."

The client's negotiating tactic was a familiar one. First, raise the agent's expectations of doing the deal. Then, at the last minute, undercut his confidence by appearing to entertain an attractive competitive proposal. Our hero, so desperate that he could hardly think, failed to grasp that these people were testing him to find out how many more concessions he could be pushed to make. In short, the client invented his own highly effective scenario for the occasion.

The prospective client, seeing that Covey's agent was simply reiterating the terms he had already negotiated over a long period, albeit with an eye toward the other's concerns, relaxed his tough stance, "stood up in the middle of [the] conversation," and casually accepted the deal in the middle of phoning his wife, to the agent's understandable bewilderment ("I was totally dumbfounded").

You need not be a cynic to see that in the agent's cutthroat world of high-stakes transactions, nothing happens neatly or predictably. Least of all do things go our way because we commit ourselves to acting out predigested, feelgood management formulas. Covey's interpretation of his "seek first to understand" example is disingenuous because he reduces the ploys and stratagems, the thrust-and-parry, the deviousness and sheer *theatrics* of deal-making to a simplistic paradigm. Not to be too dogmatic about it myself, I would agree that there are situations that call for listening before talking, but decidedly not this one.

Even without having direct access to the participants in the deal described, I would defend my made-up version of events as being more probable than Covey's, if only because I have no theory of behavior to vindicate and no rules to verify. But even if I embraced the notion of "empathic listening," I would bet that *this* client did not *want* to be understood; *his* only concern at the time was getting some last minute concessions. Put another way, the agent only imagined he was handling the client à la Covey. When push came to shove, this client was handling *him*.

Again, to be fair, I readily concede that Habit 5, Seek First to Understand, Then to Be Understood, makes good common sense: In general, everyone wants to be understood, so it is to our advantage to listen. Yet it is clear to me that businesspeople prove themselves highly effective precisely because they turn this principle on its head when the occasion requires it. Friends of mine who regularly do real estate deals on behalf of their firms cite occasions where, knowing exactly what they want, they will settle for nothing less and, therefore, make no effort to understand, let alone accommodate, the other side's needs. To do so would be to weaken their position. The idea is to deal from strength, or at least to create the *impression* that you are dealing from strength.

Which brings us full circle to David Mamet's most effective salesman, Richard Roma. Like many such people, Roma operates by instinct and street smarts. He is expert at sizing up his dupe and going in quickly for the kill. A woebegone individual drinking alone in a booth in a local Chinese restaurant tells him all he needs to know to bring the man into his confidence. An artist at improvisation, Roma launches into a monologue that defies Covey's mandate to listen first and talk afterward. And yet, in his inimitable way Roma "hears" his man perfectly. His gutter gossip, his insistence on breaching life's constraints, and his apparent mastery of life's contingencies add up to a big deposit in this individual's Emotional Bank Account. Roma has "listened" empathically.

In fact, he goes Covey one better. Roma shows Lingk he understands him, but really wins him over by liberating the man from himself. In one of *Glengarry's* most telling moments toward the end of the play, the office manager inadvertently ruins the deal Roma has made with Lingk, whereupon the latter, now off the hook, confesses to the salesman, "I know I've let you down. I'm sorry . . . Forgive me." How potent Roma's approach has been! He has made his dupe beholden to him! And the beauty of all this showmanship is that Roma (as opposed to the actor playing Roma) has done it without a script, without knowing how things will play out (in every sense of that term). The whole scene in the Chinese restaurant, while carefully contrived by the playwright, has an impromptu quality about it. It is designed to convey as vividly as possible the ingenuity with which a salesman turns a sense of the occasion, of the "moment," to advantage. We are left with the impression that a great salesman like Richard Roma never plays the same role twice; he is supremely flexible in that he can adjust his style to the most varied scenarios.

Still, we might argue that what happens on the stage in the playing time of about seven minutes or so is exaggerated or improbable, however accurate Mamet's ear for colloquial language may be. I am inclined to agree. For sheer outrageousness, this scene from *Glengarry* has no parallel in the fictions of business. Only, I believe, in real life.

Breaking the Rules: Highly Effective Salesmen in Real Life

Roma's monologue has a special resonance for me since it conjures up characters from my own business experience whose methods of making a sale I would otherwise think unorthodox, if not eccentric. One of them, a salesman whom I shall call Martin, worked for a prominent textile firm for many years before retiring with the best sales record in the company's history. As an individual, he was not likable. An intellectual with an overbearing, abrupt manner, Martin did not suffer fools gladly. With his customers he was incorrigible, browbeating them in his impatience to get an order and then to have it written on his terms. And if he wasn't bullying them, he was patronizing or overfamiliar in his attitude, often calling his contemporaries "kid." In a perverse kind of way, his manner endeared him to customers.

For Martin, listening to his customers and trying first to understand their needs was irrelevant and a waste of time. Instead, he would tell them what *he* wanted from *them*. Invariably they agreed because Martin left them no other choice. (Of course, it helped to have a thorough knowledge of his *customers'* businesses.) As a salesman he was as obnoxious in his way as Richard Roma—and equally effective. The point here is that he made no effort to leaven his approach and contain his nastiness. Instead, he *used* his more notorious traits to advantage. Most good salespeople trade on their strengths. Martin traded on his shortcomings as an individual. As a result, he was the best example of the art of selling by intimidation I have ever seen in action.

For me, though, the closest approximation to Roma's extemporaneous style was a former Maidenform salesman in charge of the company's sleepwear division, introduced as an extension to Maidenform's intimate apparel business in the 1970s. John's success was grounded in his contempt for the traditional rules of his craft. The company has always fine-tuned the selling skills of its sales force, one of the most respected in the industry, by adapting some of the classic techniques for its purposes: Listen first and talk later; attune your pitch to your customer's special needs and problems; anticipate objections if possible; develop general benefit

statements; and—the *bête noire* of mediocre salespeople—
never forget to close the sale.

John would have none of that. Like Roma, he was a
master of improvisation. His cardinal principle of salesmanship was: Never stop talking. And the natural corollary
to that was: Never talk about what it is you are actually selling. In fact, John, again like Mamet's Roma, proved that
closing a sale depends on how well you practice the arts of
distraction and irrelevance. With buyers from all over the
country present in our New York showroom to see the new
Spring or Fall line, John, instead of dutifully cataloguing
the features and benefits of the sleepwear line, would draw
on his wealth of personal stories, anecdotes, quips, and
jokes, blending them together to give the impression of an
improvised scenario.

You might well hear about his last trip to Cincinnati or
Minneapolis, where—can you believe it—he ran into Julie
Christie in the elevator. Or about how Hurricane Hortense
nearly swept away his waterfront house in Westport; or
about the time he found himself unattended at a popular LA
restaurant because the staff were all hovering around Sean
Connery at the next booth; or about how his daughter's ballet lessons paid off in her selection as a member of the corps
de ballet in the local *Nutcracker*; or about all of the above,
in no particular order. Most of it was folderol, but the buyers
were invariably enraptured because this was selling as theater, a tour de force of irrelevance and distraction by an
actor who had unerring instincts for his audience. What is
more, even with a roomful of people, John had the ability to
focus on each buyer in turn, in such a way as to make her
feel like the most important person in the room.

What John knew, of course, was that the buyers came to market week wanting to be entertained, to be wooed. There was always a tremendous air of excitement in his pitch. Part of it was body language, part of it was his dapper appearance, part of it was unswerving eye contact with the most important people there. But the real trick, John's stock-in-trade, was to keep the words flowing at all costs and somehow impart the same charged significance to everything he said, no matter how trivial. It was nonsense, but it was calculated, inspired nonsense.

I should add that the customers who over the years had had enough exposure to John to know very well what he was about were, not surprisingly, among his greatest fans—and best customers. John's ability to sustain his emcee role never flagged. Part of his ability to endure at such a high-powered level was a merging of vocation and avocation. John's corporate persona was indistinguishable from his real self. Whatever the occasion, social or business, *he was always selling himself*.

There was never a question about the sheer fun John had as a kind of performance artist—in life as in business. When the occasion, the "moment," calls for it, good salespeople, like first-rate artists, flout the rules and make up their own. Like great artists, too, they create a special aura, an atmosphere about themselves that is hard to define but that draws an audience in. The atmosphere that John created in the showroom nourished the perception that the current season's offerings were the most compelling creations in the world. The incoming orders after market week bore that perception out. His performances always had the quality of good theater.

In an age where computer technology has enabled more efficient business practices, John's highly personal, free-form approach to selling may seem to be a throwback to a bygone era. Today's salespeople are armed with computers to expedite seasonal planning, monitor sales, and apprise store managers at a moment's notice about the status of deliveries. What a boon for customer service!

Yet the use of the computer can sometimes obstruct building relationships with customers. A sales manager who reported directly to me grew so enamored of his desktop computer and the wonders it could perform that when customers came into his office, they found themselves talking to an executive sitting at a 45° angle to them, his eyes glued to the account information on the screen and his hands poised on the keyboard. There was no information or piece of data relevant to the account that he could not summon up in a flash. He had all the answers, this product of the information revolution.

Did the computer, then, enable him to handle his accounts more efficiently? Absolutely. Did our high-tech executive make stores *want* to do business with the firm? No way. Why should they when there was no spontaneity, no human pulse, no extravagant word or gesture that might prompt a buyer (I once saw it happen) to toss her order form at John after one of his improvised scenarios and let *him* fill in the numbers. If I were charged with making salespeople highly effective, I would order *Glengarry Glen Ross* in bulk, hold a seminar on selling as theater, and show them how to seize "the *moment*" before turning them loose.

Now it is certainly true that as legitimate businesspeople we cannot condone the kind of sleazy dealmaking that

Richard Roma pulls off. My point is simply that, as a primer on salesmanship as well as on survival in an ultracompetitive environment, *Glengarry Glen Ross* is tough to beat. Without cheating our customers the way Mamet's real estate salesmen do, we can appreciate the tactical value of generating images and illusions that tap into people's needs as potential consumers. On a grander scale, we shall see how merchant-bankers, movie stars, advertising executives, and empire builders succeed in promoting themselves, their services, their brands, and their great schemes in a culture where image is everything.

2

SELLING ON A GRAND SCALE: PLAYING TO AN IMAGE-CONSCIOUS SOCIETY

Mr. Melmotte was . . . certainly a man to repel you by his presence unless attracted to him by some internal consideration. He was magnificent in his expenditure, powerful in his doings, successful in his business, and the world around him therefore was not repelled.

Anthony Trollope, *The Way We Live Now*

It would be hard to overestimate the effect that the selling of image and illusion has when it reflects the values of a business-driven society. What applies on an individual level also operates throughout the culture as a whole. In this connection, we need only remind ourselves of the significance we have always attached to "public relations"—the business of image-making and manipulating people's perceptions of companies, brands, and CEOs (not necessarily in that order of importance). Recent newspaper features have picked up on the public's new interest in CEOs as cultural icons. The anonymous grey men who ran great corporations a generation ago have given way to more visible and colorful individuals. Indeed, many companies are judged on how singular an image the CEO projects.[1]

Nowadays, there is as much interest in Bill Gates and Jack Welch as unique personalities as there is in Microsoft or General Electric, the companies they manage. Similarly, media moguls like Stephen Spielberg, Rupert Murdoch, and Michael Ovitz sometimes command an image as celebrities comparable to that formerly enjoyed only by movie stars themselves. Ovitz's fall from grace at Disney has been likened by one Hollywood biographer to a Greek tragedy (notwithstanding Ovitz's $90 million severance package).[2] A more visible example of image-making is the new mural of Murdoch's fingerprint in the lobby of a new building on Murdoch's Twentieth Century Fox lot in Los Angeles. At 36 feet high, the fingerprint has an unmistakable symbolic value: "You might say he's pointing the way," according to the artist Murdoch commissioned to do the piece.[3] Equally telling, I think, is that the mural proclaims the business tycoon's self-image as a superstar in his own right, comparable to Shirley Temple, Will Rogers, and others depicted on a 1935 mural of Fox stars elsewhere on the studio lot. Isn't it conceivable that Murdoch might some day be known as the man who gave us all the Finger?

Which brings us to that great American business model, the "self-made man." Perhaps no image in American business is more revered or more misunderstood than that of the "self-made man." The popular prototype is the individual who takes advantage of the singular opportunities America offers to go "from rags to riches." Most people associate this phrase with Horatio Alger's 1867 novel, *Ragged Dick*, the story of a shoeshine boy literally dressed in rags who rises in the world through hard work, thrift, and honesty.[4]

Contrary to popular belief, Alger's real goal for his hero was not riches but respectability. Though Alger's hero does eventually become wealthy, money is less important to him than the approval of society. Living hand-to-mouth, Dick at one point offers to be a tour guide for a rich man's nephew, for which service he receives four dollars. Yet his reaction is not so much relief from the constant specter of hunger as "a new vision of respectability . . . owing to his recent acquaintance" with the rich boy. For Alger's hero, hard work, thrift, and selflessness are important in themselves, but the ultimate value of these virtues for Ragged Dick is that they will assure him of being held worthy of others' respect. At the end of the story, Dick's crowning achievement in his own eyes is to have transformed himself into a gentleman, Richard Hunter, Esq. The *image* of the gentleman that the former shoeshine boy projects is what really counts:

> Dick's great ambition to "grow up 'spectable' " seemed likely to be accomplished after all. (*RD*, 131)

My definition of "self-made people" is more literal and in fact owes more to Alger's model than to the traditional rags-to-riches stereotype, which is probably more a romantic myth than anything else. I am thinking specifically of individuals who succeed in making themselves over, who successfully create images for themselves that generate positive perceptions on the part of society, especially the people whose good will and patronage they depend on for their livelihoods. This type of individual is neither peculiar to American business nor to modern times. The self-made person is indigenous to a society driven by individual entrepreneurship and the profit motive. One familiar example is six and one-half centuries old. I have in mind Geoffrey Chaucer's profile of a self-made English merchant in *The Canterbury Tales*. This work was written during the late-fourteenth-century when a new merchant class was gradually taking hold in a world traditionally dominated by the Church and the landed classes.

Geoffrey Chaucer's Self-Made Merchant

Geoffrey Chaucer, son of a London wine merchant, Controller of the Custom and Subsidy of Wools and Hides in London, Clerk of the King's Works, and poet by avocation in the third quarter of the fourteenth century, knew merchants well—both as individuals and as international traders and financiers. His portrait of a merchant is one of a group of his portraits of contemporary Englishmen and women ranging from knight to nun, from physician to cook, and from friar to miller. Chaucer brings them together as storytelling companions on a pilgrimage from London to the shrine of Saint Thomas à Becket at Canterbury Cathedral. In the General Prologue to *The Canterbury Tales*, Chaucer casts himself as a fellow pilgrim, a modest but gregarious soul who takes it upon himself to meet and record his impressions of each pilgrim. What results is an apparently random assortment of observations on what his fellow travelers looked like, what they wore, and what they said. From these profiles, Chaucer the pilgrim-poet is able to suggest something of the person behind the pilgrim.

In the case of his merchant, no pilgrim reveals at once so much and yet so little of himself:

> A Marchant was ther with a forked berd,
> In mottelee, and hye on horse he sat;
> Upon his heed a Flaundryssh bevere hat,
> His bootes clasped faire and fetisly.
> His resouns he spak ful solempnely,
> Sownynge alwey th'encrees of his wynnyng.
> He wolde the see were kept for any thyng
> Bitwixe Middelburgh and Orewelle.
> Wel koude he in eschaunge sheeldes selle.
> This worthy man ful wel his wit bisette:
> Ther wiste no wight that he was in dette,
> So estatly was he of his governaunce
> With his bargaynes and with his chevyssaunce.
> For sothe he was a worthy man with-alle,
> But, sooth to seyn, I noot how men hym calle.

[There was a merchant with a forked beard. Dressed in rich multi-colored fabrics, he rode on a high saddle, wearing a beaver hat from Flanders and boots that were fastidiously clasped. He spoke his mind with great aplomb, always directing attention to his multiplying profits. He wanted the seas between Middleburgh (Flanders) and Orwell (England) protected at all costs. He was adroit in trading in foreign currency. This worthy man was good at living by his wits: no one would know if he were in debt, so self-assured was he in bargaining and doing deals. Surely, he was a worthy man in all respects—to tell you the truth, though, I don't know his name.][5]

The individual Chaucer twice deems a "worthy man" without even knowing his name is first and last one who cultivates and even lives for appearances. Everything in his bearing, manner, speech, and dress suggests someone who wants above all to be *thought* respectable and prosperous. Along with the poet-pilgrim, we see this merchant exactly as he wants us to see him. The forked beard; the rich, colorful garb; the fashionable imported Flemish hat; and the neatly clasped boots all bespeak fastidiousness and dignity. Quite literally from top to bottom, this has to be a person of consequence. Even the merchant's saddle is custom-made to elevate him on his horse as he rides.

To be sure, the merchant's manner and conversation are at one with his designer-level dress and personal accouterments. How skilled and self-assured he is in steering the conversation to his ability to increase his profits. In fact, the merchant's zeal in "wynning" makes him the earliest practitioner on record of Stephen Covey's Habit 4: "Think win-win."

Why, we might ask, does Chaucer's merchant take such pains to cultivate an image of respectability for himself? To a great extent, he is an individual formed by the exigencies of a business that by its very nature is erratic and unpredictable. There is the constant threat of pirates stealing the cargo in which he may have tied up his cash. No wonder the merchant wants the Crown to safeguard the commercial sea-lanes between England and Flanders. Today, the merchant's concern about pirates might be a source of entertainment, until we are reminded that piracy (of intellectual property) remains one of the most troublesome problems in today's global economy.

There is also the effect of volatile interest rates on his profit margins as well as fluctuating rates of exchange in European markets. The merchant, who must borrow heavily to finance his business, is at the mercy of his creditors, on whose goodwill he depends. These are pressures that contemporary international traders know all too well. The contingencies of his calling require the merchant to convey the kind of impression we need to deal from strength. We may not warm instinctively to self-promoters like this man, but we cannot help noticing them. First impressions are lasting ones.

One measure of the merchant's success in shaping others' perceptions of him is that he has managed to impress Chaucer as a "worthy man" without revealing a thing about himself personally, not even his name. We react, as Chaucer does, to the *image* of the man, not to the man himself. Exactly the merchant's intention. Here is a self-made individual who has mastered the fine art of selling himself to the world while keeping everyone at arm's (horse's?) length. A "worthy man" indeed. Like a seasoned actor, he is careful to avoid overexposure and therefore chooses his public appearances with care. What better way to make the world hold him in high regard than to take part in a pilgrimage to a saint's shrine?

First Impressions: The Modern Merchant-Banker

And what of this merchant's twentieth-century heirs? Some years ago an acquaintance who worked for one of Wall Street's venerable merchant-banking houses invited me to have lunch with him and a managing partner of the firm. Normally I would not have wasted my time with a "get acquainted" lunch. In this case, though, I accepted the invitation, partly because my friend insisted there would be no special agenda, and partly because I was curious.

In a sense, I felt as though I were entering a theatrical set for what I can only describe as a temple of finance: high vaulted ceilings, marble floors, wood paneling, ancient roll-top desks, a hushed, discreet atmosphere, a long corridor that made me feel somehow diminished, a slightly musty smell that doubtless carried over from the last century. The place exuded propriety and respectability. Instinctively, I checked to see that my tie was properly knotted and that my chin was up. If someone had called me to attention, military style, I would surely have assumed the position. There are times when even CEOs feel, as one of Jane Austen's chastened heroes puts it, "properly humbled."

Untoward things always happen under such circumstances. Availing myself of a nearby men's room just before meeting the managing partner, I accidentally cut my right forefinger on the edge of the towel dispenser. The bleeding was not easily stanched, and I tried without success to leave the injured member out of the handshake. The managing partner was too tactful to let on.

Urbanity was the essence of this man. He was impeccably tailored and accessorized. And his appearance was at one with his manner. I remember very little of what he said about the great ventures—joint and otherwise—which his venerable firm had financed, or about how much money it had made for its clients and itself. Strangely enough, what I do remember—and that most vividly—is comparatively insignificant. There was a pair of weighty, elegant cufflinks in hammered gold on meticulously turned, striped French cuffs. They were impossible to ignore, since their owner positioned his elbows and hands, tent-fashion, on the table, so that the cufflinks, symmetrically aligned, were on view throughout our lunch. From behind this arrangement came a sonorous, subtly modulated voice that I had heard elsewhere—on the stage, maybe, or in a broadcasting studio.

When all was said and done, the managing partner, for all of his well-turned—and well-tuned—phrases, really had no financial services to offer that his competitors could not. But the cufflinks and voice, inseparable from one another, are with me still. And despite a natural allergy to smooth talkers, I did what he wanted me to do; when I returned from lunch, I told our CFO to call this individual should the need ever arise. Clearly, his performance had struck me. Here indeed was a "worthy" man in all respects—though, like Chaucer's worldly merchant, his name escapes me.

Two Self-Made Women

For some, the art of dazzling potential customers seems to come easily, especially if they are professionals in the performing arts who just happen to be women appealing to masculine sensibilities. In the case of Arlene Dahl, a Holly-

wood icon turned businesswoman, I confess to being virtually presold.

The first act of this command performance really had its
beginning at least 45 years ago at the Saturday matinee
movies where I was a regular. Arlene Dahl was firmly
ensconced in my personal pantheon of great stars during that
era. Who, over a certain age, doesn't recall her flaming red
hair and peaches-and-cream complexion, enhanced by glori-
ous Technicolor, as she played the role of the swashbuckling
Errol Flynn's captive princess? (I must add, in retrospective
protest, that this was before movie-theater entrepreneurs
diluted the mystery and romance on the giant screen by
scrapping rococo marquees, plush velvet hangings, loges and
balconies, and chopping their theater buildings into nonde-
script multiplexes.)

Act Two. About ten years ago, I received a call at my
office from a woman who said she represented Arlene Dahl
and wanted to know whether Maidenform might be interested in discussing the possibility of becoming the licensee
for the former actress's new business, a line of apparel. At
the time, company policy was not to entertain proposals of
this kind, but this selling approach was cleverly orches-
trated. Would I take the time to meet with Miss Dahl personally? Prompted mostly—OK, *solely*—by my memories, I
agreed to an appointment.

Act Three. I was not disappointed. Talk about selling as
theater! Forty years or so had dimmed neither that fair complexion nor the flaming tresses. In all other respects the
Miss Dahl of the 1990s preserved my timeless image of her
by sheathing herself all in black, wearing oversized dark sun-
glasses, and positioning herself against the large plate glass

window in my office, so that I couldn't see her clearly for the glare. She was shrewd in another way, too. She let her agent do all the talking for her while she smiled at me—composed and inscrutable. The Arlene Dahl I knew—the *only* one I knew—remained intact. Unfortunately—or fortunately, if you look at it sensibly—I found no way to justify a decision to pursue Miss Dahl's proposal. Sometimes, good business sense does prevail, however shakily.

The second self-made woman I have in mind is purely fictional, but very real. A sense of the "moment" prompted Maidenform and Ogilvy and Mather Worldwide, Inc., our advertising agency in the early 1990s, to invent our own brand icon. In 1992, Ogilvy created an innovative 30-second TV ad for Maidenform intended to reinforce our national advertising focus on the value of the Maidenform brand for American women rather than on specific product features which vary from season to season.

To reflect a widening distribution from department stores to mass merchandisers, the agency came up with a new star: an all-American Everywoman. As in all of our previous commercials from 1987 on (see Chapter Four), this ad used our product only as a point of departure for a larger brand message. It began, "This is the bra. . . ." Then, with a twist on the familiar nursery rhyme, "The house that Jack built . . . ," the ad, in a quick succession of miniscenes, told a story about a young mother who prepares to go out to a local PTA meeting:

> This is the bra . . . that goes under the sweater . . . which is worn by the woman . . . who attends the school meeting . . . where she speaks her piece . . . which causes the vote . . . that throws the bums out . . . and makes way for

a set of reforms so popular . . . the school is renamed in her honor.

Here, indeed, was a self-made woman in her own self-created scenario. In the climactic scene of this drama of Everywoman as heroine, the camera stays in back of the woman as she "speaks her piece" to great acclaim, and the arrogant bigwigs on the dais go poof! before our eyes. As the newborn star flashes a dimpled smile in her glory, the voice-over at the end of the ad states, "Maidenform. What's *your* lingerie doing for *you?*"

Through this and other ads on the same theme, the executives we worked with at Ogilvy dramatized Maidenform's belief that for today's women anything is possible. This image of unlimited self-realization is what the ad conveyed—leavened, to be sure, by a healthy dollop of humor.

For us to appreciate fully the Ogilvy ads, we must look at the commercials that dominated the lingerie industry at the time and continue to do so today. In fashion magazines and Sunday supplements, we invariably see perfectly formed models staring into the middle distance, their visible imperfections air-brushed away. We and the agency felt, and market research at the time confirmed, that these synthetic images are demeaning to women and only reflect *men's* idea of what is alluring. The Maidenform ads did something much more important: They sold women on themselves.

The Maidenform ad I have described projects not an unreal image of a woman, but a situation so commonplace that most women can relate to it. A woman pulls a bra out of her drawer to get ready to go to a school meeting. True, the ad spins off into fantasy, but the element of fantasy is anchored in everyday, recognizable reality and seasoned with a wit that implicitly respects rather than insults women's intelligence. Which brings us back to where we started. Whether with T-shirts or with bras, it is the fiction that matters most.

Selling a Grand Illusion: Anthony Trollope's *The Way We Live Now*

Are there any limits to what impresarios of the art of selling can achieve, given the right circumstances and the right audience? The fictions of business bear enduring testimony to the power that great salespeople have when they fabricate images and illusions so universal in appeal that they can grip an entire culture. Anthony Trollope, one of the great Victorian novelists, shows how influential such individuals can be when a society is predisposed to be sold.

Though regarded today as one of Trollope's best novels, *The Way We Live Now*, published toward the end of the novelist's career in 1873, received generally poor reviews, a sure sign that Trollope accomplished what he set out to do—namely, to chastise his fellow countrymen for their lack of honesty and responsibility in their dealings with one another. Few areas of society escaped Trollope's satiric pen, from the moneyed and titled classes in Victorian London to self-aggrandizing publishers and journalists who could be bribed by hack novelists to write glowing reviews of their latest novels.

Trollope's novel revolves around a fraud perpetrated on a large scale. At the center of the book is an immensely wealthy financier named Melmotte. For such a prominent character, we know surprisingly little. Trollope tells us only that he is a European and not an Englishman, and that he has an awesome reputation as a financier, someone to whom people entrust their money for purposes of investing it and reaping a significant rate of return.

When the novel opens we see Melmotte flaunting his wealth. His opulent way of life attracts the cream of English society to him. In conjunction with his American partner, Melmotte successfully launches his grand scheme: a railroad that will stretch 2,000 miles from Salt Lake City to Vera Cruz, Mexico. Wealthy and not-so-wealthy Englishmen eagerly buy shares in Melmotte's company on the basis of his guarantee that their investments will quickly multiply in value.

It is obvious to us from the very beginning, of course, that the principals in the great South Central Pacific and Mexican Railway haven't the slightest intention of ever laying down one yard of track. The object is to sell shares in this transcontinental enterprise to as many English baronets, earls, and dukes as possible and to pocket the proceeds, all the while giving assurances that proper interest will be paid to stockholders of record.

This plot would hardly seem plausible, perhaps, were it not that, in the years just before Trollope wrote his novel, there were similar scams in England and France perpetrated on an unsuspecting public. According to Professor John Sutherland, an expert on Trollope, these may well have provided the inspiration for the Melmotte scheme. There was the Interoceanic Railway in Honduras masterminded by a notorious financier by the name of Charles Lefevre, in which British public figures were implicated. There was also the Transcontinental Memphis-Pacific Railway Company launched by a General Fremont in New York, who pocketed the funds garnered from gullible French financiers he prevailed on to fund the scheme. Thus the scheme and schemer invented by Trollope had ample precedent in recent business history. The Melmotte story has the ring of truth.

As a novelist first and chronicler of the times second, however, Trollope has other fish to fry. Like the best storytellers, he is able to make the improbable all too real. In the unfolding of incident and character, Trollope shows exactly why his elusive financier is able to pull off such an astonishing large-scale coup with such ease, and to make it a far greater success than even the great man himself could have envisioned.

Paradoxically, it is the sheer outrageousness of Melmotte and his schemes that makes him so plausible as a swindler. That no one seems to know him or anything about his past is part of the image that this merchant-prince cultivates. (How cunningly, we may recall, Chaucer's merchant protects himself against the overly curious.) Trollope intentionally keeps Melmotte's background mysterious to emphasize the impression he makes on the rich and famous, the people who can be counted on to finance his operations. Indeed, the awe with which society regards him is directly proportionate to how little it knows about the financier. There is always a calculated unreality, even an element of fantasy, about the man.

As the novelist well knows, a society driven by material values alone is one that will be inordinately impressed by appearances. Only a few pages into this teeming novel, we are given a description of Melmotte's house being set up for a ball:

> The large house on the south side of Grosvenor Square was all ablaze by ten o'clock. The broad verandah had been turned into a conservatory, had been covered with boards contrived to look like trellis work, was heated with hot air and filled with exotics at some fabulous price. . . . The house had been so arranged that it was impossible to know where you were, when once in it. The hall was a paradise. The staircase was fairyland. The lobbies were grottoes rich with ferns. Walls had been knocked away and arches had been constructed. The ball had possession of the first floor and ground floor, and the house seemed to be endless.[6]

Trafficking in illusion can go no further than this. That the place has a positively disorienting aspect to it is at one with Melmotte's financial legerdemain. The premise to the financier's grand strategy is that appearances count for everything. After all, what is the financier really selling but worthless paper? And the more magnificent the appearance, the better. His duplicity notwithstanding, Trollope's character is in a direct line with Chaucer's richly caparisoned merchant, the man who strives, above all, to be *thought* respectable.

An indispensable part of Melmotte's carefully staged image is the cultivation of English royalty. Lord Alfred Grendall, a penniless and feckless member of the aristocracy, is a man whose favor it behooves Melmotte to curry. How adroitly the financier handles him, flattering him while holding him hostage by assuming his debts:

Melmotte was very anxious to get into Lord Alfred's club, The Peripatetics. It was pleasant to see the grace with which he lost his money, and the sweet intimacy with which he called his lordship Alfred. Lord Alfred had a remnant of feeling left and would have liked to kick him. But there were his poor boys and those bills in Melmotte's safe. And then Melmotte lost his points so regularly, and paid his bets with such absolute good humour! (*WLN*, 36)

While he may caricature the titled classes (what writer ever missed the chance to do that?) Trollope is careful to show Melmotte, the supreme confidence man, as smart enough not to overreach himself in buying his way into society. When the Prince himself appears at his party, Melmotte is shown not to be a fool:

[He] "understood not only that it had been thought better that he should not speak to the Prince, but also that it might be better that it be so. He could not have everything at once." (*WLN*, 42)

On the other hand, Melmotte knows that if he were to represent his commercial enterprises on anything but a grand scale, he would be suspect. As a superior writer, Trollope underscores this point by showing how people are drawn to the financier *despite* their distaste for him personally:

. . . Mr. Melmotte was a big man with large whiskers, rough hair, and with an expression of mental power on a harsh vulgar face. He was certainly a man to repel you by his presence unless attracted to him by some internal con-

sideration. He was magnificent in his expenditure, powerful in his doings, successful in his business, and the world
around him therefore was not repelled. (*WLN*, 80–81)

This passage says as much about the character of the
society that adores Melmotte as it does about the financier
himself. As manipulative as he is, Melmotte owes much of
his success to a tacit collusion between him and his backers. Despite their suspicions that Melmotte's scheme
"was . . . built upon the sands," they cling to their image of
him as "a tower of strength." These suspicions grow as Melmotte's machinations become more transparent in the latter part of the novel. Yet Trollope is quick to show that his
backers' need to believe in the illusion of fabulous wealth
that the financier has conjured up for them overrides their
common sense. At one point, Melmotte nearly makes a
fool of himself defending his great enterprise at a venerable
men's club:

> He was not eloquent; but the gentlemen who heard him
> remembered that he was the great Augustus Melmotte,
> that he might probably make them all rich men, and they
> cheered him to the echo. (*WLN*, 89)

When prompted by greed and pandered to by an impresario
of illusion, the will to believe sweeps all before it:

> Wonderful are the ways of trade! If one can only get the
> tip of one's little finger into the right pie, what noble
> morsels, what rich esculents, will stick to it as it is
> extracted! (*WLN*, 89)

Under the scenario that Melmotte has conjured up, the honest and the dishonest are undifferentiated in their common understanding that their "fortune was to be made, not by the construction of the railway, but by the floating of the railway shares."

In the flush of his unexpected series of coups, Trollope's financier overreaches himself, done in, finally, by an overpowering sense of his infallibility as a master salesman. In this, he is like many otherwise brilliant commercial magnates we read about almost daily, whose indestructible belief in themselves leads first to spectacular success and then to a reckoning, as the old Quakers used to say. I draw one such example from the business annals of our day—one that indirectly involved my own business, and one also that shows a remarkable similarity to the short, happy life of Trollope's fictional antihero and the setting in which his financial misadventures ran their brief, dazzling, and ill-fated course.

Trollope Revisited: The Way We Live Now

Just as Trollope took his cue from current events, so the chronicles of business in our time may be said to imitate the old fictions. If we were to advance the clock 100 years to the present and comment about the way we live now, it would be fairly easy to show how life imitates art. The great purveyors of illusion keep working their magic on a grand scale in our time as well.

I have in mind the way in which a Canadian financier, Robert Campeau, managed by way of a leveraged buyout (LBO)—the business of taking over other businesses—to assume control of and then to put at risk some of the most prestigious department stores in America during the mid-eighties, with consequences that are still being felt in the retailing and manufacturing industries. Here, too, was a "self-made" man adept at creating an outsized persona for himself that by its sheer scope and scale drew people to him and compelled their confidence in him. Here, too, is the story of how the greed and gullibility of people in high places helped them ignore their experience and common sense in an environment increasingly characterized by a sense of unreality. It is a story worthy of great fiction.

Robert Campeau was a real estate developer from Canada who made his fortune in the 1970s by way of housing projects in Ottawa and, later, office buildings and apartment high-rises in Toronto. The son of a blacksmith, he came from a very remote and parochial part of Canada, but rose above his modest circumstances through a combination of business acumen, vision, daring, and tenacity.

In the mid-eighties, Campeau decided that he wanted to expand his real estate empire to the United States and, with the help of an investment counselor in New York, became interested in the possibility of buying some shopping malls that were then owned by the Allied stores.

According to John Rothchild's *Going for Broke*, a fascinating account of Campeau's rise and fall, the developer became intrigued by the leveraged buyouts that continue to engage the financial community.[7] Prominent among these was the Macy's LBO of 1986. Out of the blue, it seems, Campeau decided that he wanted to do more than buy up American real estate; he wanted to take over the four-billion-dollar Allied department and specialty store empire itself. His rationale was an illusion propagated on a grand scale: the notion that managing department stores was tantamount to managing real estate.

"Wonderful are the ways of trade." Trollope could not have invented a more felicitous phrase to describe the speculative fever of the 1980s, so similar to that which flabbergasted the writer in the 1870s. Inside of six months from the point when he first convinced himself that he could take over and *manage* a retailing empire with which he was totally unfamiliar and which was ten times the size of his own company, Campeau had accomplished what he set out to do. He was the proud owner of Allied Stores.

How was this possible? On the face of it, the Campeau scenario was as improbable as anything Trollope ever concocted in his fictions. A Canadian real estate developer comes out of nowhere with designs that are transparently preposterous. Commercial and investment bankers, in turn, collectively loan him 2.5 billion dollars, staking their money and reputations on a venture that anyone with eyes to see would run from in a flash.

Part of the answer is obvious: The prospect of huge upfront management fees on the part of the financial community and law firms coupled with an opportunity to establish themselves and their organizations as key players in the new and highly lucrative mergers and acquisitions market was too good to pass up. As in Trollope's London, speculative fever was running high. Whether that speculation took the form of a transcontinental railway or an LBO is really immaterial. The point in each case is that new ways of getting rich quickly were at hand, and they fueled the desire of all kinds of investors to get in on the ground floor.

Still, the acquisitive impulse of investors, financiers, and companies can account only in part for the ill-advised Campeau acquisition of Allied and, soon afterward, of the Federated stores—an $11 billion deal—that few really believed would succeed. The two once healthy retailers went bankrupt under their new CEO in about the same time it took Campeau to acquire them. Only the selling of an illusion of wealth and power on a grand scale can account for why so many astute and experienced people proceeded like lemmings into a man-made sea and brought traditional department-store retailing to grief.

There can be little doubt that Campeau himself, besides being an extraordinarily ambitious individual, was a master at self-promotion. In *The Way We Live Now*, Trollope outdoes himself in describing the parties Melmotte throws to create the illusion of great power and wealth, and to curry the favor of royalty. The air of fantasy and unreality in Trollope's description may seem a fabrication of escapist fiction. Campeau, in fact, goes Melmotte one better. He, too, gave lavish parties to promote himself, to validate his claim to be ranked among the rich and famous. I am especially impressed by an account in the Toronto *Life* magazine describing Campeau's bash after the completion of his Toronto waterfront project. Apart from the extravagant trappings, Campeau arranged for the Royal Regiment Guard of Honor to be present, so that he could review the troops as though he were a member of the royal family.[8] Even the great Melmotte was discreet enough to stop short of such antics.

The outlandishness of the fictitious Melmotte and real-life Campeau, however, is an essential part of the image they project. Ironically, it is what draws people to them. In both cases, the sheer magnitude of the enterprise combined with the confidence each man exudes causes sophisticated businesspeople who should know better to suspend their common sense and judgment.

There is a sad irony inherent in Campeau's financial hi-jinks. Here was a master salesman who understood the importance of image making in convincing rational people to suspend their judgment and, by the end of the day, happily spend more than they had bargained for. Now it was precisely the strategy of American department stores from the beginning of the century to bedazzle customers like Theodore Dreiser's Sister Carrie with images of abundance and luxury, allowing them to revel in a theater of consumption. Yet Campeau was too heavily constrained by the financial burdens he had assumed in his massive acquisitions to realize his plans for carrying this grand retailing tradition forward. Faced with an impossibly high debt, Allied and Federated were forced to slash prices, service, and overhead costs to survive financially. In doing so, they lost customers, forcing further self-destructive cost cutting. Established national brands like Maidenform, in turn, suffered treatment in many department stores as a cut-rate commodity at the point of sale. What was now to distinguish the department stores from the national chains and discounters? For these retailers and the brands whose image they helped nourish, the experience was one from which, I believe, they have yet fully to recover.

And what of the redoubtable Robert Campeau? Despite his empire's bankruptcy and his subsequent disappearance from the American retailing scene, he is still making front-page headlines in the *Wall Street Journal*. Now in his 70s,

Campeau has embarked on one of his most ambitious and daunting schemes yet: the development of a huge home-building project in Berlin, where local residents have nick-named Herr Campeau "Mr. Wonderful." Why? Because he "always says how everything is wonderful."[9]

Masters of the Universe: Selling in Cyberspace

I am sometimes bemused by all the talk nowadays about the endless possibilities for selling goods digitally on the infor-mation highway in cyberspace. The most sought after com-modity so far seems to be information itself. Lots of it.

I am watching Bill Gates on TV. He is informing a rapt group of United States governors about the advantages of the Internet for consumers. He is low-key and matter-of-fact about his plans for intergalactic communication. A very effective salesman. Gates is making the point that a con-sumer walking into an automobile showroom today has an edge in the old negotiating game, since he or she now knows what the *dealer* paid for the car he's trying to sell. Just so.

And yet . . . I don't quite see it. A *sale* still has to take place at some point, and I would bet that a superior sales-person still has the edge. I say *superior* salesperson advisedly because he or she knows that the price customers will pay is merely a function of the value customers put on what they are buying, whether T-shirts, real estate, or intercontinen-tal railway shares. And that perceived value will go up, I maintain, not in proportion to the amount of information at the customers' disposal, but according to how effectively the salesperson has mastered the art of selling to image-conscious customers.

The most effective entrepreneurs understand that one of the realities of life in business is that the world of make-believe is all important. The truth is that people need fiction in their lives. If we wear our consumer hats, we can understand this. In the world of make-believe, there are no rules, no ready-made formulas. But for the self-made individual, the individual who recreates him- or herself as the occasion warrants, who makes customers form new images of *them*selves, there are endless possibilities for creativity and improvisation, just as there are in the performing arts.

The fictions of Chaucer, Trollope, and Mamet belie the notion that the information revolution, so-called, will make traditional ways of selling and buying obsolete (or reduce our vulnerability to con men.) Profound *technical* changes are surely upon us, but the contemporary, real-life analogues to the characters and situations in these fictions indicate that salespeople in cyberspace, looking to conquer the universe, will have to tailor their approaches to profound *human* needs and impulses that have resisted change for centuries.

3

MAINTAINING INDIVIDUALITY
IN CORPORATE LIFE

"Not finding yourself at the age of thirty-four is a disgrace!"
Arthur Miller, *Death of a Salesman*

T he fear of losing our individuality in choosing a corporate career has always been part of American business mythology. The postwar image of enforced
conformity, the Man in the Grey Flannel Suit, still haunts
us, though few remember the 1956 novel by that name. My
own view is that an individual's fear of becoming a corporate
clone begins and ends with the individual. Unless people
intentionally subordinate themselves and their personal
values to the prevailing company culture, the idea that they
will somehow be swallowed up by the company culture is
baseless.

Put in a positive way, I would insist that the key to maintaining a sense of ourselves as individuals in corporate
life is self-awareness. Individuals who are self-aware are also
self-empowered because, knowing their limitations as well

61

as their capabilities, they take their corporate lives into their own hands. Rather than wait for authority to be bestowed, they create their own challenges within the structure of the company and find ways to meet them. Frequently, the classic conflict between the individual and the corporation obscures a more fundamental struggle between the individual and himself. Indeed, I would argue that the most troublesome constraints in corporate life are not imposed by the corporate culture; they are the constraints we impose on ourselves.

Through the wrenching internal struggles of their central characters, the fictions of business demonstrate how deeply our individuality in corporate life is rooted in self-awareness. Tom Rath, the Man in the Grey Flannel Suit, intentionally submerges his identity in an organization-man persona until he is forced, inevitably, to reexamine his values and be honest with himself. Arthur Miller's Willy Loman is nominally a salesman, but in reality he is an escape artist bent on avoiding himself at all costs. By living vicariously through other people, both real and imagined, Willy becomes in every sense a nonentity. Unlike Tom Rath, he persists in being dishonest with himself, the terrible consequences of which Miller's play sets vividly before us. In direct contrast to Willy Loman is Charles Gray, the successful investment banker in John P. Marquand's *Point of No Return*. Instead of trying to escape from himself like Willy, Gray never stops searching within for his authentic self—what he stands for as an individual. His is a struggle to liberate himself from a life that he feels is "contrived" and that stamps him as an "assembly line executive."

The Illusions of Conformity: Sloan Wilson's *The Man in the Grey Flannel Suit*

Sloan Wilson's novel, published in 1956, is perhaps the most enduring of all the fictions of business—for the wrong reasons. Most people tend to remember the book for its symbolic title, not for its characterizations and plot. The Man in the Grey Flannel Suit has become an American icon for corporate conformity. Wilson's plot and his characterization of Tom Rath, though, are more complex and instructive than commonly thought.

The novel's hero, Tom Rath, returns to his family from the war seeking two things: a comfortable living and a restoration of order in his life after the chaos of the war. In pursuit of these he leaves his job as an underpaid foundation executive going nowhere fast and lands a job as a midlevel public relations executive for a large broadcasting firm in Manhattan.

Tom's initial assignment is to write speeches for Ralph Hopkins, the company president, who asks him to draft a speech rallying public support for his pet project: a mental health program. Though accomplished at speech writing, Tom finds Hopkins rejecting successive revisions of the speech. What has gone wrong? All along, Tom has been cynically assuming that his boss's interest in mental health must be a publicity stunt designed to enhance Hopkins's personal image and to put a respectable face on United Broadcasting to compensate for the company's low-grade but profitable TV programs. He has therefore larded the speech with platitudes about the importance of mental health and studded it with catchy slogans ("Our wealth depends on mental health"). Though Hopkins isn't sure himself of how to cast his forthcoming speech to a gathering of the medical profession, he is rightly uncomfortable with Tom's superficial and insincere PR approach.

Wilson is careful to show us how much Tom's cynicism costs him. The mythological way to succeed in business is to try to please your boss, to tell him what he wants to hear— or more accurately, to tell him what you *think* he wants to hear; in *The Man in the Grey Flannel Suit*, this is exposed as self-defeating. It becomes clear, midway through the novel, that Tom has sold his boss and *himself* short.

> That Tuesday morning Tom perfected the latest draft of the speech he was writing for Ralph Hopkins. The whole text, which was now about thirty pages long . . . had come to seem a sort of penance from which he would never escape, an endless tract, a meaningless life-work. (MS, 146)[1]

The feeling of entrapment in meaningless work is the price Tom Rath has to pay for doing the kind of work that does him no credit and in which he doesn't really believe. Although he collects himself and resolves to show "initiative on this mental health project," it is obvious that he is still fundamentally dishonest with himself:

> . . . he dictated a memorandum . . . requesting permission to visit the state mental hospitals and several leading psychiatrists to gather information about mental-health problems. He added that he was planning to get together

a bibliography on the subject—he thought that sounded quite impressive. (MS, 149)

The turning point in the career of the Man in the Grey Flannel Suit occurs when Hopkins, feeling that Tom is becoming stale, asks another executive to rewrite the speech. Hopkins subsequently asks Tom for his opinion of the new version; and Tom, who is now able to look at the speech objectively for the first time, realizes that it is riddled with slogans and that it offers no concrete proposal for improving mental health. For a moment Tom imagines himself saying to his boss:

> *"I'm sorry, but I think this speech is absurd. . . . If you want to form a mental-health committee, why don't you find out what needs to be done and offer to help do it?"* (MS, 193)

Wavering, he reverts to self-deception, and somehow it doesn't feel right:

> I should quit if I don't like what he does, but I want to eat, and so, like a half million other guys in grey flannel suits, I'll always pretend to agree, until I get big enough to be honest without being hurt. That's not being crooked, it's just being smart. . . . But it doesn't make you feel very good, Tom thought. It makes you feel lousy. (MS 193–194)

What we want to happen—that the *real* Tom Rath stand up—does in fact happen, not because a popular novelist wants to gratify his readers, but because Sloan Wilson knows that people who are fundamentally honest and whose self-respect is at stake cannot hide from themselves indefinitely. In urging Hopkins to propose practical ways to initiate a mental health program rather than simply reiterating how important it is, Tom gains his boss's respect. He tells Hopkins what the chief executive has actually *needed* to hear all along. It is at this point that Hopkins enjoins Tom to rework the speech in a way that satisfies them both.

Wilson does not let his newly reformed hero off so easily, though. As an astute writer, he knows that honesty, too, can be an exacting virtue. Just as we want Tom to come clean with his boss and, more critically, with himself, so we want his honesty to be rewarded; it is, but not exactly in the way we would expect. Hopkins does honor Tom's integrity by giving him a chance to advance in the firm as a line executive. The days of live TV broadcasts are now numbered, and it appears that Hollywood will become the new base of operations for the firm. Hopkins offers Tom the job of setting up a "separate but affiliated organization" in California. On the face of it, this is a corporate careerist's dream. Yet Tom Rath balks. He knows that getting a new operation off the ground will require the kind of sacrifice of time and family life that he is not really prepared to make.

In a second and even more momentous bout with his conscience, Tom realizes that if he refuses the offer, Hopkins might turn on him ("This is like petting a tiger"). But he also recognizes that Hopkins is a "guy who can't be fooled." His answer to the chief executive's query, "Don't you want to learn the business?" is one that I have found people in corporate life to echo frequently, though more in private than in public:

"I don't think I do want to learn the business. I don't think I'm the kind of guy who should try to be a big executive. I'll say it frankly: I don't think I have the willingness to make the sacrifices. . . . I want the money. . . . But I'm just not the kind of guy who can work evenings and week-ends and all the rest of it forever. I guess there's even more to it than that. . . . I can't get myself convinced that my work is the most important thing in the world. . . . And I know that to do the kind of job you want me to do, I'd have to be willing to bury myself in it, and, well, I just don't want to." (MS, 263)

Respecting his honesty once again, Tom's boss offers him a middling staff position in the East—but not before turning on him momentarily and giving him a tongue lashing:

Suddenly Hopkins whirled and faced him. "*Somebody has to do the big jobs!*" he said passionately. "This world was built by men like me! To really do a job, you have to live it, body and soul! You people who just give half your mind to your work are riding on our backs!" "I know it," Tom said. (MS, 264)

Hopkins is right, of course, as any CEO will attest. The point Sloan Wilson is making in this novel is that self-awareness and personal integrity are not easy to sustain, but they are preconditions for anyone choosing a corporate career. The critical point for Tom Rath is that he gets what he wants for himself. The only constraints in his corporate career are *self*-imposed.

Thus *The Man in the Grey Flannel Suit* is not what its title alone suggests. There is a difference between what the Man in the Grey Flannel Suit represents and what Tom Rath, the individual, represents. The novel itself is about an executive who changes from a passive anonymity to an individual who gains the self-awareness necessary to make the decisions that do him honor. Tom's own self-recognition at the end of the novel attests to the magnitude of the change:

> I was my own disappointment. I really don't know what I was looking for when I got back from the war, but it seemed as though all I could see was a lot of bright young men in grey flannel suits rushing around New York in a frantic parade to nowhere. They seemed to me to be pursuing neither ideals nor happiness—they were pursuing a routine. For a long while I thought I was on the side lines watching that parade, and it was quite a shock to glance down and see that I too was wearing a grey flannel suit. (MS, 284)

The vital thing about Tom's progress from mindlessness to *self*-consciousness is that it is personally liberating. He is no longer on the fast track, but it is essential for him that he has *chosen* not to be in that position. In making that critical choice when it needed to be made, Tom Rath has become a self-empowered individual. Sloan Wilson always makes it clear that the company has never imposed itself or its values on *him*. That is never an issue. Tom Rath's central conflict always lies within himself. The story of how he overcomes his own perceived need to conform provides the enduring interest of *The Man in the Grey Flannel Suit*.

The Self-Empowered Leader

As Tom Rath demonstrates in his struggle with himself, self-effacement may be a virtue, but not in corporate life. There is no such struggle in his boss's case. Quite the contrary. From the beginning, Hopkins, the company president, typifies individual self-empowerment. "This world was built by men like me!" he exclaims. And who would gainsay him? To a large extent he does carry the organization, and he knows it.

The novel is somewhat schematic in that it opposes Hopkins's compulsive attention to the business and consequent alienation of his family to Tom's insistence on a life apart from the business at the expense of a senior management position. You can't have it both ways, the novel suggests. You can, of course, have both, as the many CEOs who manage to balance their personal and corporate priorities know full well. The key point here, though, is that in Hopkins's mind there is no wavering; his is a single-minded commitment from the start. He is the soul of ambition; that is the way he is made. There is no agonized soul-searching for him as there is for Tom because he knows who he is and what he wants from the get-go. To see Hopkins in a failed light simply to validate Tom's decision not to ignore his family is not to give Hopkins and men like him their due. *"Somebody has to do the big jobs."*

The point here is that Hopkins's self-command as the leader of his organization is never in doubt. It is his absolute faith in himself that is the key to his ability as a leader. I hesitate to use such words as "ego" and "ambition" in describing people like Hopkins because of their negative connotations for most people. How many news stories are there about business tycoons who fail because they let their outsized egos get the best of them and cloud their judgments? And how few are there about the role of a good, healthy ego in the making of a self-empowered leader?

It is difficult to convey the kind of personal impression truly self-empowered leaders make, except to say that you never doubt that you are in their presence. Likewise, you never doubt that what they say about themselves is true, however outrageous it may sound out of context. My favorite personal example of the self-empowered individual is that of Ida Rosenthal, a founder of Maidenform.

When I first met Ida Rosenthal over 35 years ago, the company she had helped to found in 1922 had long since entered the annals of American popular culture. It was she and her partner who, with Ida's husband William, developed what became known as the first uplift bra—a garment that was to change the flat-chested "flapper" look and become an indispensable part of women's wardrobes worldwide. In the apparel industry, Mrs. R., as she came to be known, was legendary. She combined an astute marketer's understanding of women's attitudes and needs, a financier's flair for a profitable deal, and a flamboyant charm. She was a genius at selling herself and her company.

My first meeting with this woman was not propitious. I was supposed to pick up my blind date (later my wife Catherine) at her grandmother's apartment. Ida Rosenthal, a diminutive woman, answered the door and showed me in. One of those awkward silences followed the usual pleasantries. To make conversation, I made a leading remark based on my (then) sketchy knowledge: "I understand you're with Maidenform," I said. My mistake, an honest one of course, was the "with." As in one of those animated cartoons, Mrs. Rosenthal suddenly sat up to an unimaginable seven feet (while I shrank to nothing) and replied, with perfect equanimity, "I *am* Maidenform." After a very brief pause to let the truth of this statement sink in, we both laughed.

I can never think about maintaining individuality in corporate life without recalling this incident. Newscasters nowadays like to talk about "defining moments." For me this was surely one of them—literally. For clarity of *self-definition*, Mrs. Rosenthal's "Maidenform, c'est moi" would be tough to beat. If anyone knew what she was about, this self-empowered leader certainly did. Her remark encapsulated two qualities which she played off one another like a virtuoso: imperiousness and charm. She let me know where she stood, but at the same time she let me off easy.

In her business relations, Mrs. Rosenthal was equally formidable. It is easy to forget how singular an individual she was from our vantage point today. In the early 1920s through the 1930s, she pioneered the role of a self-empowered female entrepreneur and executive. What she had going for her in this enterprise were a fierce independence and a willingness to take calculated risks. This was the same woman who, at the age of 18, had come to America alone; disdained factory work—disdained working for anyone else, in fact—and instead bought a sewing machine on time and established a reputation as the best dressmaker in Hoboken, New Jersey, by the age of 23. This was the same Ida Rosenthal who ignored the advice of friends and family when she subsequently invested almost her entire savings of $4,000 to become a partner in Enid Frocks, a fashionable boutique on West Fifty-Seventh Street in Manhattan. And it was this New York dress business out of which the idea for the uplift bra was to emerge and eventually to lead American women's fashion in a new direction.

Ida Rosenthal's understanding of what women wanted grew naturally out of her own consciousness of herself as a model of femininity. During the "flapper" era, she and her partner had the common sense to realize that women really didn't want to look like boys. Their brassiere was specifically designed to create a soft, rounded look that emphasized the body's natural contours. As she later stated, "Nature made women with a bosom. So why fight nature?" What started out as an idea that might have been appealing only to the fashionable clientele Mrs. Rosenthal had initially catered to in her dress business, became an idea that, as she had rightly envisioned, commanded universal appeal.

Of course, it was one thing to come up with a great idea. But great ideas are ineffectual in business unless someone has the will and sense of leadership to execute them. The business that was to become Maidenform was an extension of Mrs. Rosenthal's qualities as an individual. To her advantage, she possessed an intimate—I use the word advisedly—knowledge of every phase of the business from finance and marketing to production. She was comparable to a great conductor who knows exactly what she wants from each orchestral section, from strings to percussion, based on a knowledge of what each section is capable of individually and the kind of effect they can produce together. She was the compleat executive.

In conjunction with her drive as an executive, Mrs. Rosenthal used her femininity to create an aura that captivated customers and colleagues alike. For many, she had the authority of an oracle. I am particularly impressed by a UPI report from 1959, under the heading, "Brassieres could help ease tension." The reference is to Mrs. Rosenthal's remarks as the only woman member of a U.S. trade delegation to Russia. Alluding to East-West tensions at the time, she was quoted as saying:

> "If they [Russian women] wore bras they would be happier and prettier. The men would be happier. Consequently, the whole country would be more contented and I think Russia's relations with the U.S. and the world might improve."

Breathtaking? Of course. Mrs. Rosenthal, always aware of her effect on people, was charming her audience by making a statement no different in kind from the one she would later make in my presence, only raised here to a more universally edifying plane.

For this self-empowered leader, retirement was out of the question. When in her late 70s, which is to say, her prime, she said, in all seriousness, "I didn't retire when I was 65 because I didn't have time." After all, "*Someone has to do the big jobs.*"

That a purely fictional set of circumstances could have a direct bearing on the business judgment of a practical, self-empowered leader like Ida Rosenthal may seem, well, unrealistic. Yet it is fair to say that a signal influence on her thinking at a critical point in Maidenform's history was a play about a long-time employee who is unceremoniously fired by the head of a family-run company. The employee's name was Willy Loman, and the play was Arthur Miller's *Death of a Salesman.*

A Case of Mistaken Identity: Arthur Miller's Willy Low-Man

Death of a Salesman is the best known and most hallowed of all the fictions of business. When the play was first produced in 1949, audiences were said to be so moved by the drama that at the final curtain there was a stunned silence in the theater before the first burst of applause. For Ida Rosenthal, the play seemed to justify her reluctance to effect a much-needed reorganization of the Maidenform sales force. Though schooled in the realities of developing a national brand, she was prompted by Willy Loman's desperate plight to resist temporarily any change that would cut territories and commissions. One of Maidenform's chief retail customers was similarly taken with Miller's story of a failed salesman. In his autobiography, *Timebends*, Miller relates how Bernard Gimbel, the department store owner, vowed upon seeing the play that no Gimbel's employee would henceforth be fired for age.[2] When the revival of the play with Dustin Hoffman came out in the early 1980s, I remember salespeople in our firm talking about it with reverence. Their identification with Willy Loman—the "man way out there in the blue, riding on a smile and a shoeshine"—was absolute. "There but for the grace of God go I!" is still the prevailing sentiment among all those who see Willy's death as that of just another disposable "low-man," inexorably ground up in the corporate mill.

These reactions to the play are honest enough, but I believe they have little to do with the play Arthur Miller wrote. Over the years, Willy Loman has become a universal symbol for all casualties of corporate life who are unable to adjust to changes in the way the company does business, or to compete with the company's young turks bucking for promotion, or simply to sustain their vitality under relentless business pressures. *Death of a Salesman,* on the other hand, is about a more fascinating and subtle problem: Willy Loman's failure to come to terms with *himself.* Miller's Willy Loman is a man who avoids the self-awareness required for a successful adjustment to corporate life, not to say life in general. He is a man who disables rather than empowers himself by ignoring who he really is.

It is easy as well as tempting to see Willy as a hapless victim, another case of corporate burnout. Much of what persists in people's minds about the play supports this point of view. The famous scene in which Willy is summarily fired from the company he has faithfully served for 34 years is an example. If taken out of context, as it usually is, the scene becomes an example of managerial callousness. An exhausted Willy, desperate to hold on to his job, appeals futilely to the second-generation owner Wagner, his former boss's son, to take him off the road and reassign him to a selling job in the New York showroom.

> WILLY: Look, it isn't a question of whether I can sell merchandise, is it?
> HOWARD: No, but it's a business, kid, and everybody's gotta pull his own weight. . . . 'Cause you gotta admit, business is business.
> WILLY: If I had forty dollars a week—that's all I'd need. . . .
> HOWARD: Kid, I can't take blood from a stone, I—
> WILLY: [*desperation on him now*] Howard, the year Al Smith was nominated, your father came to me and—

HOWARD: I've got to see some people, kid.

WILLY: [*stopping him*] I'm talking about your father! There were promises made across this desk! You mustn't tell me you've got people to see—I put thirty-four years into this firm, Howard, and now I can't pay my insurance! You can't eat the orange and throw the peel away—a man is not a piece of fruit! (*DS*, 80,82)[3]

These are certainly words to arouse compassion, and we can readily see why Ida Rosenthal and Bernard Gimbel were inspired to reiterate their loyalty to their senior employees. In our own time, what more powerful a scene could you pick to appeal to managers disabused of the old-fashioned notion that there is any such thing as a company's long-term responsibility to its workers?

And yet it is necessary for a proper appreciation of Miller's play to understand that this scene is not a plea for more responsible management, but the culmination of what Willy has brought upon himself. Willy's frustration as a company cast-off can induce us to forget that he himself has called the meeting with his young boss. Wagner is actually surprised to see him ("Say, aren't you supposed to be in Boston?"). Prior to this scene, Willy, who has indeed become less effective as a salesman (it isn't clear that he was ever very effective at all), has been placed on straight commission. That makes things harder for him, but it isn't as though he has been laid off. What's more, it is his wife, Linda, who has insisted that he see Wagner over Willy's own misgivings: "They don't need me in New York," he had responded to her, in a rare bow to reality.

The tragedy of this scene is that Willy deliberately ignores his own best counsel and demeans himself in the process. That is, he *allows* himself to be humiliated by refusing to jettison the illusion that the company owes him a living. At issue here is not Willy's failure to conform to what the company requires of him, but his refusal to recognize what he has made of *himself*.

"We've got quite a little streak of self-reliance in our family," Willy insists to his "barely interested boss." Would that it were so! It is clear to us, though, that Willy is not his own person, and never was. In fact, he has no real identity, no self-awareness apart from the people he has set up in his mind as rugged individualists. Any individuality he may claim for himself, in other words, is vicarious. There is his father, a sometime flute player, sometime inventor, and sometime prospector, whom Willy once had a "yearning" to follow to Alaska to strike gold. There is his older brother, Ben, a shadowy figure whom Willy conjures up whenever he needs to feed what Arthur Miller calls his "massive dreams." Ben is another pioneering entrepreneur who went to Alaska in search of gold—or was it Africa in search of diamonds?—and emerged a rich man at the age of 21.

Finally, there is the bizarre Dave Singleman, who, Willy says, convinced him that "selling was the greatest career a man could want." And who is this inspirational figure? Why, a man who would go up to his hotel room, put on his "green velvet slippers . . . and pick up his phone and call the buyers, and without ever leaving his room, at the age of eighty-four, he made his living." This is the very figure who dies "the death of a salesman" in—what else?—his green velvet slippers "in the smoker of the New York, New Haven, and Hartford, going into Boston." As his name implies, the mythical Singleman is the singular individualist that Willy, with no inner resources of his own, can only *imagine* himself to be.

Miller has Willy Loman make it self-evident that all his life he has imagined himself to be someone he could never possibly be. As reality closes in on him, Willy stakes more and more on his son Biff's ability to preserve the great Loman legacy: He will charm the buyers and make the world love him. Biff, of course, crumbles under this burden and meets with the inevitable rebuke from Willy: "Not finding yourself at the age of thirty-four is a disgrace!" The irony is telling. Nothing Willy says in the play better underscores his own lack of self-awareness.

That Willy feels burned out is not the problem, only a symptom of it. His real dilemma is that the barriers he has erected to guard against real self-awareness are becoming harder and harder to sustain. When his sympathetic brother-in-law, Charlie, offers the desperate Willy a job, he refuses it. "I've got a job," he lies. "When the hell are you going to grow up?" Charlie replies. Like the unreformed Tom Rath, Willy remains dishonest with himself, and he too feels trapped ("The way they boxed us in here. Bricks and windows, windows and bricks"). He is the great *negative* example in the fictions of business of the self-empowered individual.

If Miller, who is sometimes accused of pontificating, has a point to make here, it is that people like Willy Loman are not victims of impersonal corporate manipulation with little personal choice in their fates. Just after Willy is fired, the bewildered salesman is given a piece of common-sense advice by his brother-in-law Charlie's son, now a successful lawyer:

> BERNARD: . . . sometimes, Willy, it's better for a man just to walk away.
> WILLY: But if you can't walk away?
> BERNARD: I guess that's when it's tough. (*DS*, 95)

For Willy to "walk away" at this point would be to show an unwonted self-awareness. And yet there would be no better way, ironically enough, for Willy Loman to assert his individuality in corporate life than by withdrawing from it gracefully.

Linda Loman's famous and often quoted defense of her husband is frequently taken out of context as the playwright's defense of the common man against an impersonal system. In fact, her plea echoes that of Willy when he is dismissed:

> LINDA: . . . I don't say he's a great man. . . . He's not the finest character that ever lived. But he's a human being, and a terrible thing is happening to him. So attention must be paid. He's not to be allowed to fall into his grave like an old dog. Attention, attention must finally be paid to such a person. (*DS*, 56)

I have never taken these words at face value. They are lines in a play spoken by a wife who nourishes her husband's illusion that he is being victimized. In fact, I find these lines more descriptive of her than of Willy. It is Willy, after all, who has been digging his *own* grave in *Death of a Salesman*.

The same point holds true for another, equally miscon-strued set-speech: Charlie's closing eulogy at Willy's funeral.

> CHARLIE: Nobody dast blame this man. You don't under-stand: Willy was a salesman. And for a salesman, there is no rock bottom to the life. He don't put a bolt to a nut, he don't tell you a law or give you med-icine. He's a man way out there in the blue, riding on a smile and a shoeshine. And when they start not smiling back—that's an earthquake. . . . Nobody dast blame this man. A salesman is got to dream, boy. It comes with the territory. (*DS*, 138)

Like much funeral oratory, Charlie's speech bears little resemblance to reality. It deliberately echoes Willy's own gospel of success as built on personality—the art of being "well liked." Charlie, a successful businessman who has tried but failed to get Willy to be honest with himself, knows bet-ter. Deliberately whitewashing Willy's flaws for the occasion, Charlie attempts to lend dignity to Willy's life as a salesman.

Yet Miller takes pains to qualify Charlie's eulogy by framing it with the remarks of Willy's son Biff: "He never knew who he was. . . . the man didn't know who he was." Having finally cast off the heroic mold into which his father had cast him, Biff can now see himself and, by extension, his father with new eyes. Miller's *un*sentimental drama is about a man who has failed himself. In the terms that this play sets forth, maintaining our individuality in corporate life is, above all, a matter of paying attention to *ourselves* when such attention needs to be paid. Cultivating self-awareness is a stringent discipline, and "it comes with the territory."

I am convinced that the more self-aware we become as managers, the more alert we become to how we should handle failed employees like Willy. *Death of a Salesman* makes it clear that Howard Wagner, the second-generation owner of the business, has long ignored his veteran salesman in Boston. That Willy's sales have been poor and are getting worse is obvious. The only action Wagner has taken, though, is to limit Willy to what he can make on straight commission. In doing so, Wagner has done his salesman more harm than good. By carrying Willy along over the years, Wagner has helped him nourish his illusions rather than ground him in reality. Maybe "promises" *were* made by Willy's former boss, Wagner's father. But why hasn't management leveled with Willy over the years? Only when a desperate Willy himself forces the issue does Wagner finally tell him he's finished:

WAGNER: I don't want you to represent us. I've been meaning to tell you for a long time now. (*DS*, 83)

"I've been meaning to tell you. . . ." For me, these words epitomize negligence on the part of management. Most companies tolerate their Willy Lomans because executives procrastinate. They avoid letting the employee know up front that he has no future with the firm. An example from my own company comes to mind.

Many years ago, Maidenform's national sales manager hired a young man (let's call him Paul) in an entry-level position covering a small account territory ("Mom and Pop" stores). The sales manager, pleased with his new hire's results, took him under his wing and eventually promoted him to key account salesman servicing major department stores. In this capacity, Paul continued to perform well. He was aggressive; he worked hard, and he established good working relationships with his accounts. Two or three years after he had begun working for Maidenform, he was promoted to district sales manager in his territory.

As it turned out, Paul proved to be a poor manager. But because the national sales manager had adopted Paul as his protégé, he went out of his way to protect Paul. Instead of taking him to task, he found ways to shield Paul's incompetence. Under the circumstances, Paul must have been made to feel that he was doing an adequate job and that his future was secure.

In fact, Paul's lack of managerial skills were the least of his problems. As a seat-of-the-pants operator, he was unable to adapt to change. New, more sophisticated methods of tracking rates of sale, identifying placement opportunities, and preparing seasonal plans were beyond him. His continued reliance on selling the old-fashioned way, "riding on a smile and a shoeshine," hurt him. Still feeling obliged to shelter his man, the national sales manager "solved" the problem by demoting Paul from district manager back to key account salesman. This move only made matters worse. As a manager, Paul had been able to rely on a few star salesmen to make the sales goals for his district. Now on his own, he began to lose a significant amount of business to competitors who took advantage of up-to-date selling techniques.

In hindsight, it is clear that management made the classic error of promoting Paul to the level of his incompetence (per the Peter Principle). The more serious error in my view, though, was in demoting him to the level of his incompetence. Being an ineffective manager is one thing; being resistant to fundamental industrywide changes is quite another matter. Placing Paul in an important sales position requiring flexibility and adaptability, the qualities he most lacked, was to prove as much a disservice to him as to the company.

Though Paul's deficiencies became increasingly obvious, not just to the company, but also to the retailers he serviced, the national sales manager still felt a strong personal obligation to him. Trying, as he thought, to spare Paul and to minimize the damage Paul could do in the field, he demoted him further to a territory of mostly small accounts. Paul must have been aware that he had thus come full circle, since he wound up virtually where he had begun his career so many years before!

Why didn't Paul leave the company when he saw where his career was headed? Because senior sales management made it too easy for him to stay. It rewarded the veteran salesman's years of service by giving him the option of staying on. It even found ways to justify the gap between his salary and the business he actually generated.

Under the circumstances, ensuring job security was probably the *worst* thing the company could have done for this man. People he worked with in subsequent years have told me how painful it was to watch Paul cope with conflicting emotions. Having to put on a smile and cajole buyers while despondent about his dead-end career must have been hell for him. Here we come very close, I think, to Willy

Loman's conflicted feelings that he is at once somebody and nobody:

> WILLY: Oh, I'll knock 'em dead next week. I'll go to Hart-
> ford. I'm very well liked in Hartford. You know, the
> trouble is, Linda, people don't seem to take to me.
> (DS, 36)

How did things come to this pass for Willy and for Paul? How did a company employee become simply a company fixture? Miller's play and Paul's history with Maidenform suggest that the humane and sensible action would have been to put each man on notice sooner rather than later. Wagner and Maidenform's sales manager should have helped their failed salesmen "walk away" rather than let them reach the point where they were unable to do so.

Firing someone who has reported directly to you over a certain period is one of a manager's most unpleasant tasks, and it doesn't become any less unpleasant through repetition. The longer a manager sidesteps this responsibility, the more difficult it becomes. Executives nowadays are practiced in massive downsizing, but that is a wholly different proposition. Downsizing is impersonal. As a "corporate decision," it does not require any explanation, let alone a face-to-face confrontation. An executive can blanket a division with pink slips much more easily than he can deal one-on-one with an employee who is clearly not long for the company.

Difficult as releasing an individual might be, managers do no one any favors by their inaction when the writing is on the wall. To have been honest with Willy and Paul would have helped them to be honest with themselves. To have helped them empower rather than disable themselves would have been to act compassionately. Without an image of themselves as self-dependent individuals, Paul and Willy both became nonentities in their respective companies.

The Preassembled Executive

The threat to our individuality in the corporate world is by no means confined to people like Willy Loman and Tom Rath, who are hostage to their own illusions and preconceptions. Quite the contrary: The disjunction between our dreams and reality can be particularly painful for the most apparently well-adjusted and successful individuals. The fictions of business also dramatize how competent executives lose touch with themselves precisely during those times when they appear to be most self-assured. John P. Marquand's novel, *Point of No Return*, published in 1949, the same year *Death of a Salesman* opened, probes the turbulent inner life of a successful banker searching for identity in his chosen profession.

Marquand was one of the most accomplished American novelists of the mid-twentieth century. Nowadays, his chronicles of the lives of the rich and privileged, notably *The Late George Apley* (for which he won the Pulitzer prize in 1937), may seem tame and old-fashioned. Yet Marquand's leisurely narratives are deliciously satirical in exposing the personal limitations and social constraints of pure-bred Bostonians. In *Point of No Return*, Marquand combines social satire with a penetrating characterization of a man in search of himself within a seemingly preassembled corporate life.

Charles Gray, Marquand's hero, is an assistant vice president of a bank in Manhattan, specializing in trusts and estates. His wealthy clients are particular about the way they are treated, and Gray has spent years perfecting a "priestly, untouchable, ascetic attitude" in working with them. In doing so, he suffers the occupational hazard of a "split personality," debating the "purchase or the sale of controls in business enterprises" and then returning home to decide whether he himself can afford a motor-driven lawn mower.

> At your desk, you had to be a friend and confidant, as professional as a doctor or a lawyer, ready and with an intelligent perspective for almost anything. Anthony Burton [the bank president] had once said that this attitude was one's responsibility toward society. Though personally Charles had never felt like a social worker, he felt this responsibility. He was already forgetting Nancy and the children, already assuming his business character, when he said good morning to Gus, the doorman. . . .
> (PNR, 28)[4]

From his outsider vantage point, Marquand is alert to the comic aspects of self-conscious executives like Gray and his associates. Jockeying for position, for example, has its literal as well as its figurative aspects. The location of your desk defines your status at the bank. Since Gray is only an assistant vice president, he sits "in a sort of no man's land between the roll-top desks of the officers and the smaller flat-tops of lesser executives and secretaries crowding the floor of the bank outside the cages." His desk is just inside the green rug that forms a "neat and restricted zone" for the executives. And what happens when one of the executives dies or retires? Everyone moves in a kind of preordained ritual, "like players on bases—Burton to Harry, Merry to Burton, Slade to the vacant roll-top. . . ."

Marquand's typecasting in regard to personal appearance is also unerring. His description of Tony Burton, the bank president, through Gray's eyes reflects ironically on Gray himself:

> [Burton] had that air of measured deliberation which eventually always covered the features and the postures of bank officers and corporation lawyers. He was slender and athletic, almost young-looking considering that he was close to sixty-five, though Charles could never think of him as having been a young man. Charles always thought of him as unchanging, a measured, deliberate, constant quantity, like a Greek letter in a mathematical formula. (*PNR*, 30–31)

What unsettles Gray is this very predictability, for he realizes that he, too, comes preassembled, a perfect image of a banker rather than a banker with a unique identity. He, too, has become "unchanging," a "constant quantity." Beginning his day's work, ". . . his whole mind set itself into a brisk, efficient pattern."

What increasingly distresses Charles Gray is not the daily ritual of donning his "business character," but the feeling that his life as an efficient working professional carries no real sense of fulfillment for him. Marquand keeps us guessing whether his hero will receive a coveted vice presidency, but *Point of No Return* is more than a familiar melodrama about office politics. Gray is less concerned about money or prestige than about his inability to derive personal gratification from his chosen vocation.

To find fulfillment in his work means that Gray has first to find himself. The search for personal identity, while a common theme in fiction, takes an unusual form in this novel. Contrary to the familiar coming-of-age pattern in which the insecure adolescent grows into the more self-assured adult, the problem of self-discovery for the mature Charles Gray increases in proportion to his adjustment to his life's work.

Moments of self-doubt ripple through the settled surface of Gray's existence. The sense of his life as "contrived" encompasses all his roles as husband, parent, and executive. "It's funny, when I came down there to breakfast this morning, the whole place seemed ready-made," he says to his wife on the way to the commuter train. But she is not on his wavelength. Instead she takes his remark to be a comment on her efficiency. "That isn't what I mean," says her husband. Pulling up to the station, he elaborates. Pressed by his wife to take the advancement of his career more seriously, Charles Gray reiterates that "this whole business sounds contrived." Again, she misunderstands, thinking that by "contrived" he simply means "funny":

> I didn't say it was funny . . . I said it was contrived. The little woman kissing her husband good-by. Everything depends on this moment. He must get the big job or

Junior can't go to boarding school. And what about the payments on the new car? Good-by, darling, and don't come back to me without being vice-president of the trust company. That's all I mean. (*PNR*, 14)

It becomes clear to Gray that he has to work out his problem for himself. At first, he consoles himself that everything will turn out all right if he continues to plug away at the bank. Part of his malaise, though, derives from the very virtues that serve him so well professionally. "The probity, the reliability and the sobriety that such a task [administering trusts and estates] demanded were to make his own life dull and careful." More ominously, Charles Gray finds that his own character is subsumed in a larger, impersonal corporate identity:

The Stuyvesant [Gray's bank] was the aggregate of the character of many individuals, who merged a part of their personal strivings and ambitions into a common effort. . . . In the end, no matter what the rewards might be, a part of one's life remained built into that complicated structure . . . the clerks, the tellers, the department heads, the vice presidents, the president and the directors . . . were all on an assembly line, but you could not blame the line. It was too cumbersome, too inhumanly human for anyone to blame. (*PNR*, 478–479)

Left in suspense as to his promotion, Gray tells his increasingly anxious wife:

> There's no use getting mad at a system. We're part of a
> system where there's always someone waiting to kick you
> in the teeth in a nice way. (*PNR*, 138)

The sense of entrapment that afflicts Willy Loman and
Tom Rath also weighs heavily on Charles Gray. By contrast,
however, Gray is a man who has never faltered or let himself
down in his exemplary career as a banker, so his recurrent
"malady" is vexing to him.

> He knew the symptoms well enough. First there was a
> period of general uneasiness about nothing in particular,
> and then a growing illusion of being hemmed in, followed
> by a desire to escape, and finally an indescribable sense of
> loneliness mingled with a sort of deep self-pity which he
> particularly hated. . . . The only thing to do was to tell
> himself to behave, that he would be better in a little
> while. (*PNR*, 140)

Things don't get better though. Gray comes across an
old friend who has published a sociological study of Clyde,
Massachusetts, the town where Charles Gray grew up. In its
compartmentalization of social groups from "lower-lower" to
"upper-upper," the study echoes Gray's gnawing feeling that
his life has been preordained:

> He could see the passionless exactness of that scientific
> picture, stripped of sentiment's flattering lights and
> shades. . . . Its inhabitants [Clyde's] moved into a pattern
> like bees in a hive. . . . There was the individual's unknow-

ing surrender to the group, and the unthinking desire for order. (*PNR*, 147)

The now upwardly mobile New Yorker longs to shuck a life that is "enclosing him in impersonal mediocrity," a life that Gray feels is not his own:

> Please, God, his mind was saying, get me out of this. Please get me out of this. (*PNR*, 144)

On a business trip to New England for his bank, Charles Gray decides to revisit Clyde in an effort to understand himself from the perspective of his past. Entering into his central character's thoughts as Gray travels north, Marquand gives us a long flashback on Charles's relationship to his father, John Gray.

This retrospective portrait of his father as a failed businessman is not a pretty one. From his mature vantage point, Charles realizes that his father was a negative model for him in almost every respect. Reckless in his investing, self-pitying, and sanctimonious, John Gray railed against the "system" that purportedly did him in. Compared with his father, Charles Gray is purposive, ambitious, and conservative in his judgments. Indeed, he would seem to have done well by himself despite his father's example.

Does Charles Gray's latter-day reflection on his father's limitations make him more philosophical, more accepting of the life he leads? Not really. In his final view,

> . . . freedom of choice was limited. He could see himself hurrying, always hurrying, and he would be hurrying

again tomorrow, back to Nancy and the children and
back to taking care of other people's money. It was not
what he had dreamed of, there in Clyde, but if he had to
start all over again he would not have acted differently.
(PNR, 527)

As a seasoned novelist desirous of satisfying his readers but
also conversant with life's arbitrariness, Marquand makes
sure that things do turn out all right for Gray (he gets the
vice presidency he deserves), but the author qualifies this
happy outcome by leaving his central character as unsettled
as before. In a telling scene at the end, Gray, summoned by
the bank president, suspects he will not get his promotion
after all. Since it appears he has nothing to lose, Gray experiences a giddy moment of freedom in which he feels that he
is no longer hostage to the bank (or to himself). Ironically,
his feeling of personal liberation ends precisely at the
moment when he learns of his advancement. Now he has
reached "the point of no return," and the sense that his
whole career has been preprogrammed makes him feel the
"same old weight, and it was heavier after that brief moment
of freedom." Gray reflects that his new status was what he
"had dreamed of long ago, and yet it was not the true texture
of early dreams."

Good writers know that human problems do not go
away of their own accord and that life does not yield up
comfortable resolutions. What Charles Gray sees from his
new, loftier vantage point is not new at all: The "whole
thing was contrived . . . an inevitable result, a strangely hol-
low climax." There is no more poignant example of how
unrewarding success can be.

Creating "Flow" in the Corporate Workplace

It seems to me that Marquand's postwar novel has particular relevance at a time of high employee and management turnover, for it implicitly addresses the issue of how today's corporate managers and tomorrow's managers can strike the often elusive balance between committing themselves to their companies and looking out for their own well-being. Charles Gray is conscientious to a fault, but his white-collar assembly-line syndrome suggests a deadening routine, aggravated by his feeling of being locked inside his multiple personae. "Priestly" toward his clients, ambitious for the sake of his family, socially conscious in relation to the community his bank serves, this well-adjusted executive is a model of *self*-effacement.

Were we to lift Charles Gray from the pages of *Point of No Return* and advise him on how to mitigate his sense of entrapment in his work, we might indeed suggest that he set aside some quality time to cultivate personal interests. In my experience, successful senior executives with the most pressing corporate responsibilities have the most varied range of outside pursuits. If we attend to what really troubles Charles Gray, however, we must reckon with a more fundamental issue: "Is the work we do intrinsically satisfying?" "Is it fun?" The question is as pertinent for those whose "business character" operates on automatic pilot as for those who hold, as I do, that engaging in truly challenging work is imperative for both corporate managers and for the people they manage. I use the familiar term "challenging work" in a strict sense. In my own managerial lexicon, it has to do with the concept of "flow," as articulated by Mihaly Csikszentmihalyi in his fascinating book, *Flow: The Psychology of Optimal Experience*, which appeared in 1990.[5]

To be in "flow" is to be in a situation where a given challenge is precisely equal to your ability to meet that challenge. This condition can apply to a range of human activities. The most dramatic example is the feeling of flow athletes sometimes get when, pressed by competition, they enter a "zone" in which they find themselves performing at or beyond their peak over an extended period. Recently, I read an account of a promising young basketball player who scored a phenomenal number of points in a game. When asked about his unprecedented performance, he simply replied that, when he had the ball in his hands, he was absolutely sure of making a basket. Of course, physical skill is a prerequisite, but the singular element here was a mindset that seemed to guarantee amazing results.

Less dramatic but equally unforgettable is the feeling of flow intellectual challenges generate. This is something I know from first-hand experience. In the middle of writing my doctoral dissertation, I once experienced flow in much the same way I suspect the basketball player did. One late afternoon I happened to be working on a vexing problem that involved an analysis of a group of characters in a medieval play based on Biblical themes. On the face of it, this is not a particularly stirring topic. Yet it was *my* topic, and while only a medievalist might deem it worthy of hard mental labor, I can hardly convey the sense of excitement I felt when, all of a sudden, my thoughts began to come together in perfect order, and my writing, sentence by sentence, then paragraph by paragraph, followed suit. I was as sure of getting my analysis right as the basketball player was of bagging three-pointers at will. My writing took on a rhythm and clarity that I knew would continue as long as I was in my zone, on a high, in flow. I didn't dare leave my desk, lest the spell be broken. If this sounds like something magical, it was. I experienced a peculiarly liberating feeling during this period, released from everything that might inhibit or limit my mastery of the problem I faced. The challenge of the problem at hand activated mental resources equal to that challenge—resources I didn't even know I had. I felt blessed.

My account would seem to stray far from the corporate workplace. I'm not so sure it does. I believe that generating flow is vital to executives responsible for avoiding an "assembly line" mentality of the kind that must eventually produce stagnant organizations. Granted, professionals like Charles Gray are essential to the life of any business. Executives like him are paid to maintain a solid and unchanging image for the sake of their clients. Yet it is clear to me that Gray is disaffected because he lacks the kind of challenge that can tap otherwise dormant resources and enhance the quality of his working life.

In corporate life, the principle of flow is the same as in any other activity. It behooves us as managers and executives to create for *ourselves* the kinds of challenges conducive to flow. Bringing your untapped resources into play to meet special challenges sounds like a wonderful thing to do, but is it really doable in a large organization where the routinizing of work lends order and regularity to complex business processes? Csikszentmihalyi's answer to that one is simple (though not easy). Creating flow in the workplace is less a question of the "inherent characteristics of jobs" than of "how one perceives opportunities." He goes on to cite examples of those who "saw challenges in tasks that most people would find dull and meaningless. Whether a job has variety or not ultimately depends more on a person's approach to it than on actual working conditions."

A friend of mine, Kevin Brine, whose job as a senior vice president of a research and asset management firm working with private and institutional clients is similar to that of Charles Gray, provides a good example of a creative approach to business. Though one of Kevin's primary functions, dealing with private clients, is similar to Gray's, he perceives his job as stimulating rather than dully repetitive. Interestingly enough, what originally drew him to the firm he has been with for many years was not asset management as a business calling but the intellectual challenge this kind of work posed for him.

Kevin's expressed conviction is that business in general and the culture of his business in particular are inherently intellectual. He even goes so far as to describe the investment management field as iconoclastic by nature. Far-fetched? Hardly—more like common sense when you think about it. Kevin believes simply that to find opportunity in undervalued securities, an investment manager has to see the world differently from others. The decision to buy a particular equity that others are deciding not to buy often flies in the face of orthodox thinking or precedent. In short, *how* this corporate individualist perceives his job is what counts for him. We are surely at a far remove here from the world of Charles Gray—and from Tom Rath, for that matter—where there is such a strong perceived need to conform by assuming a "business character."

As you might expect, Kevin cultivates a variety of interests outside his work. As a religion major in college, he read Sanskrit. He still writes extensively. One of his works in progress is a book about his relationship with his father (coincidentally, what so much of *Point of No Return* is about). Kevin sits on hospital and school boards and is one of the prime movers of an organization that treats children with AIDS. I cite these humanistic and humanitarian interests not simply to state that they are interesting or admirable in themselves, but to show how they nourish his creativity at work.

Although a study of world religions may sound like an unlikely background for investment management, the philosophical bent which that discipline requires was especially useful to him in formulating a distinctive marketing strategy for Kevin's firm, Sanford C. Bernstein and Co. In relating to prospective clients, he felt that his built-in competitive advantage was not an ability to hard-sell his product ("We guarantee performance," etc.) so much as a rarer talent for building a large customer base by articulating the management philosophy of his firm. In providing this service, Kevin felt that he helped create a sense of a brand for his organization. And there was an added value in this for him personally. In continuing to use his special skills to advantage, Kevin has become, in Czikszentmihalyi's words, "more of a unique individual, less predictable, possessed of rarer skills."

Not everyone, of course, is fortunate enough to find a home in a company that values this kind of creativity and individuality. I am particularly impressed by the management philosophy of Zalman C. Bernstein, the founder and chairman of his firm:

We try to convince everyone in our organization to reach for the stars—no matter how menial or repetitive their tasks may be, we try to give meaning to their lives when they work at Bernstein. Be it a receptionist, or our chief investment officer, working at Bernstein is an exciting experience. My job is to keep it that way. To keep an atmosphere where ideas are constantly flowing. . . .[6]

Exactly how I would approach my own job at Maiden-form after years of immersion in university life was not altogether clear to me at the time I elected to join the business. To this day people ask me how I was able to make such an apparently radical transition. Answer: not without difficulty. It was up to me to recreate flow for myself in a corporate setting. I knew no ways to do this other than to utilize my teaching and writing skills to advantage. For example, I would like to think that writing position papers, marketing plans, and market-test analyses for the company helped make it more effective than it already was. I would like to think, too, that moderating annual executive retreats and getting executives from finance, sales, marketing, and operations to reach a consensus on company ends and means was one way of creating challenges for both myself and the organization.

For me personally, the important thing in the 20 years I worked for the company was never to lose touch with myself, with the things that irreducibly made me what I was, who I am. Accordingly, the most important challenges I encountered were not imposed from without. They were the challenges I created for myself. To keep myself honest, I prepared a personal inventory that I have continued to use as a checklist to keep myself and not my "business character" front and center. Who am I? What do I really enjoy doing? Does who I am accord with what I am doing? Am I doing it right now, and if not, why not? What do I want for myself? What do I have to do to get it? Curiously enough, highly personal questions of this sort are what keep us in flow, and serve our interest as individuals. And it is the *self*-serving individual, in turn, who best serves the company's interests.

4

OVERCOMING CORPORATE GOSPEL AND THE WILL TO BELIEVE

"I'll play it the company way . . ."

Frank Loesser, *The Company Way*

ost of us are predisposed to believe what we want to believe and to screen out what we find unpalatable. If we want something to be true badly enough, it will become true for us, even if the facts tell us otherwise. A teacher of mine used to call this trait "the will to believe," and warned that it creeps up on us unawares. Often scholars and scientists, seeking to be objective in their claims and judgments, will slight facts and even common sense trying to confirm their own ideas and theories.

Business executives and managers are likewise vulnerable to the will to believe, even though they are routinely judged by their decisions, not by their research. Corporate captains who devise "action plans" thrive on positive thinking. It is easier and more convenient for them to think about what can go right rather than about what can go wrong. Leaders are valued more for their creativity, vision, drive, and ability to inspire loyalty than for traits that can safe-guard against the will to believe, such as an innate sense of caution, a healthy skepticism, and a tolerance for construc-tive dissent.

Middle managers who aspire to leadership generally fol-low suit. Rare is the individual willing to question higher corporate wisdom. Who ever receives credit for demonstrat-ing the undesirability of launching a new service or product? Because corporate managers usually reinforce one another's opinions (though often for different reasons), company plans, once activated, acquire a momentum of their own. Of course, the force of collective action can spur implementa-tion of plans. On the other hand, ignoring signs that a pro-posed corporate strategy might well fail can be costly and wasteful. To appreciate fully how the will to believe can flourish in a business setting and what its real as well as its hidden costs can be, we should turn to the testimony offered by the fictions of business.

"Devising Good Lies": Joseph Heller's Company Men

Joseph Heller's novel, *Something Happened,* a darkly comic work among the fictions of business, demonstrates how the will to believe can grip executives and managers. This work is invaluable to us because it slices through the veneer of cor-porate life to reveal the consequences of embracing corpo-rate gospel, so often obscured by office decorum and routine.

Heller's story, set in an unidentified marketing and man-ufacturing company in an unspecified American city, appeared in 1974. This was a time when the typical Ameri-can executive was an "organization man," whose loyalty to his company and expectations of corresponding rewards was absolute. Today's world of corporate downsizing has ren-dered these traditional loyalties obsolete. *Something Hap-pened*, however, is anything but dated. It extends the theme of Heller's famous *Catch 22*—collective insanity engendered by a wartime bureaucracy—to American corporate culture in the postwar era.

Anyone expecting *Something Happened* to be a melodra-matic thriller, with money and power up for grabs, will be disappointed. There is no plot that turns predictably on the ability of an executive with a moral conscience to prevail over those who have their own rather than the company's interests at heart. Nor is there even a recognizable hero. Yet Heller concocts a story that is far more real than anything most conventional novels have to offer. Through his central character, Bob Slocum, a midlevel executive who narrates the entire book in the first person, Heller depicts the kind of workplace that nourishes faith in corporate gospel.

Bob Slocum is the consummate company man. By fol-lowing the tacit corporate requirement that executives do exactly what they are told to do, not more and not less, Slocum is a model employee. Though a middle manager in a large firm, he nonetheless has a key job: "devising good lies." In contemporary jargon, he might be called the company spin doctor. As head of the market research department, Slocum is "not expected to change reality" but to find "inge-nious ways of disguising it." Converting "whole truths into half truths and half truths into whole ones" is Slocum's stock-in-trade. If the industry data at hand reveal the company to be at a "competitive disadvantage," it is Slocum's mission to make this information palatable by recasting it.

Essential to Slocum's methods is a reliance on official government sources, such as the U.S. Census Bureau, the Department of Commerce, and the Pentagon. These give his own reports the desired credibility. Because of his talent for "disguising" reality, his work is a boon to the Sales and Public Relations Departments. Slocum's tone of voice may strike the reader as surprisingly matter-of-fact. It can only be that of a man who is accustomed to taking this kind of double-think for granted. There is nothing of sensational revelation or exposé in his narrative. This is the way things have always been, Slocum implies, and always will be. And that is so because the rest of the company also has a vested interest in the purveying of illusion:

> In fact, I am continually astonished by people in the company who do fall victim to their own (our own) propaganda. . . . Every time we introduce a new advertising campaign, for example, people inside the company are the first ones to be taken in by it. Every time we introduce a new product or an old product with a different cover, color, and name that we present as new, people inside the company are the first to rush to buy it—even when it's no good. (SH, 24–25)[1]

Shades of the emperor's new clothes! As Joseph Heller well knows, the absurd is often embedded in routine. While conventional thinking might tell us that belief in company gospel can be damaging, the reality, as Slocum is quick to perceive, is continued success based largely on the salesmen's ability to swallow whole and then regurgitate what Slocum's research concocts for their purposes:

> When salesmen and company spokesmen begin believing their own arguments, the result is [that] they develop an outlook of loyalty, zeal, and conviction that is often remarkably persuasive in itself. It produces that kind of dedication and fanaticism that makes good citizens and good employees. (*SH*, 25)

Little wonder that Bob Slocum's company "is having another banner year." For Heller to have shown his fictional company as declining in fortune because it thrives on half-truths and lies would have obscured his point that creating and sustaining proper perception is vital in corporate life. Such an enterprise can be a delicate one, of course, and the occasional glitch is inevitable. When one of Slocum's fellow spin artists starts believing his own fabrications, the result is "disastrous, for he begins relying too heavily on what he now thinks is the truth and loses his talent for devising good lies."

> 'But it's true, don't you see?' he would argue softly to the salesmen, the secretaries, and even to me . . . 'We *are* the best.' (The point he missed was that it didn't matter whether it was true or not; what mattered was what people *thought* was true.) (*SH*, 25)

". . . what people *thought* was true." This part of Bob Slocum's narrative has a special resonance for me. About the time that Heller's novel appeared, I began my career with Maidenform as a marketing manager. Having done academic research, I understood the primacy of consumer research in providing a basis for the marketing projects to which I was assigned. Little did I realize how soon I would be caught up in one of those projects whose failure derived from the very thing I had always sworn off in my own research: the will to believe. I bring it up at this point because most of us are often too ready to compartmentalize "fiction" and "real life" without appreciating how interchangeable they sometimes are.

Going with the Corporate Grain: Cost *Inefficiencies*

As a manufacturer and marketer of intimate apparel, Maidenform distributes its national brand to the nation's department and specialty stores. In the mid-1970s, the company had broadened its base of customers by concentrating on the needs of young, fashionable women. Essential to the current fashionable look in lingerie were unadorned yet colorful garments made of soft fabrics that stretched to conform to the contours of the bustline. This provided a smoother, more natural look under clothes than more traditionally constructed bras afforded. Maidenform had a number of bestsellers of this kind.

As a member of the company's marketing committee, I had been involved in the development of a new group of stretch bras from the initial concept through the execution of a full-scale consumer advertising program. As experienced marketers, we were adept at embellishing a line of existing best-sellers. This time around, our designers chose a lighter stretch fabric than the usual and added attractive lace trim to the shoulder straps to enhance the visual appeal of the garments. We were quick to bless our new creations and named them No-Show Naturals.

How could anyone not believe the No-Show Naturals, scheduled for introduction at the forthcoming intimate apparel market week, would succeed? Maidenform dominated a growing market that we ourselves had created. Retailers, anxious for their part to capitalize on the demand for stretch merchandise, felt that Maidenform was "on a roll." A national television ad promoting No-Show Naturals buttressed our confidence in the new entries. We followed suit with production estimates high enough to cover retailers' orders, as well as to supply back-up stock for the massive reorders that we were sure would follow once the initial quantities sold out.

Through a comprehensive all-out marketing and selling effort, the company secured heavy orders from retailers. Delivered on schedule, the No-Show Naturals appeared front and center on department store selling floors. Then, to our bewilderment, they failed to attract the very customers responsible for Maidenform's growth in the category of seamless stretch merchandise! The company's losses in markdowns and returns, excess inventory, and an extensive marketing campaign were substantial.

What went wrong, and at what point did it go wrong? Rounding up the usual suspects—an unpredictable marketplace, competitive initiatives, the fickleness of consumers—proved futile.

Could we blame the vagaries of the market? No: If any-thing, the demand for seamless stretch bras was surging. Had there been a shift in consumer tastes and values? No: The desirability of branded merchandise that combined a fash-ionable appearance with a good fit and comfort was the basis on which Maidenform had built its market share since the 1920s. Were there competitive challenges that we hadn't anticipated? No: Maidenform "owned" the seamless stretch business at that time. Had we done inadequate planning? Not at all: From product development and engineering to production scheduling and distribution, things had come off without a hitch. Was there simply a lack of communication among departments? No, that could not have been the problem either.

In the end, we gave up trying to determine where we lost out; the prevailing belief was simply that we needed quickly to write off this product failure and get on with it. Still, I wondered whether some research on my part might remove some of the mystery surrounding the ill-fated venture. A postmortem report I made to the marketing committee attempted to account more particularly for what went wrong, to avoid our repeating the same costly mistakes with subsequent marketing programs.

I did not have to probe very deeply. There was ample evidence suggesting that we had violated a cardinal rule of marketing: Give the consumer what she wants. The market research department had done its job well. Its timely reports to the executives on wear and preference tests with depart-ment store shoppers months prior to the launch indicated that most women were dissatisfied with the features designed to differentiate our new line on the selling floor by offering them, as we thought, attractive options in stretch merchandise. While the department store customers who participated in the tests found the new lace trim on the shoulder straps attractive, they also saw the straps as too heavy, making for an unnaturally conspicuous rather than smooth appearance under clothes, the very thing women *least* want in this type of bra.

At the same time, they perceived the main fabric of these garments as too light. Seamless garments require the use of heat to mold the cup of the bra to ensure a proper fit. The problem was that when the fabric we chose for No-Show Naturals underwent this heat-molding process, it was stretched to the point where it became sheer. And while a sheer or "see-through" look was consistent with the natural look of updated merchandise, in this case the degree of sheerness evidently crossed the bounds of consumer propriety, even for lingerie designed to look alluring.

Communication from shoppers had been clear and direct. *Our* problem was that we collectively screened out what they told us. Smitten by our own creation, we seized on those elements of the test results that confirmed what *we* thought of our Spring introductions. For overall appearance, the No-Show Naturals ranked high. For those features that women desired in updated seamless stretch merchandise, however, the ratings were poor. Ignoring these, or giving them short shrift, we filtered out what we found unpalatable in our consumers' responses. The gist of my report was that we had put more stock in what we and our retailing partners liked than in what participants in our preference tests for seamless stretch bras had told us they wanted.

The will to believe becomes virulent when a group of executives, fired by success, find reasons to feed each other's optimism. We hear so often about self-destructive conflicts within large companies between sales and finance, marketing and operations. We hear little, however, about the damage that can be done when department heads think and act as one. Product-development managers tend to applaud consumer research that confirms the potential they see in their own products and to slight research that does not. Sales managers see in such cases the probability of an easy sell and an additional open-to-buy allowance on the part of the buyers. Production managers see the prospect of increased efficiency with long runs at full capacity. Financial managers expect a high return on investment. And marketing managers see an advertising and promotional campaign that might well enhance brand equity, win prime space on retailers' selling floors, and increase market share. All kinds of sound reasons augur success for a line of products, while the specter of failure, signaled by communications direct from consumers, steadily recedes. Among the primary underlying causes of new product failures in American business is surely that companies *choose* to ignore the obvious.

To be sure, I have oversimplified the situation. Potent factors other than data from sources such as consumer research and sales analysis inform business decisions. Intangibles that are impossible to measure like experience, a "feel" for the market, taste, instinct, timing, and sometimes pure dumb luck come into play. The documentation of probable consumer dissatisfaction at the point of sale, however, hardly justified Maidenform's sizable investment in the program before seeing any evidence of sales in the stores themselves. Indeed, experience had always told us that, while positive results from preliminary wear and preference tests are unreliable in predicting winners, negative results have the accuracy of a Sibylline prophecy: We ignore them at our peril.

Why, given these uncertainties, did Maidenform not opt to postpone the introduction and give these garments the benefit of a market test under actual selling conditions? The answers we gave ourselves at the time seemed legitimate enough. We would have blunted the momentum of an innovative and (we thought) timely new product. Besides, the retailers with whom we had previewed the No-Show Naturals had promised to commit a sizable portion of their budgets to the new program. The real answer, however, was unspoken. We had presold *ourselves* on the success of the program.

It would be very tempting to claim that my report changed the way Maidenform planned new product introductions. To succumb to that temptation would be to yield personally to the will to believe. Postmortem reports like mine are unpopular because *no one wants to be reminded of failure,* let alone of his or her part in it. QED. The company was henceforth loath to commit substantial resources to an untried program; but this change of approach to new product introductions owed less to my rueful history than to an unacceptable waste of time and money. We had learned the hard way.

For some, Joseph Heller's fiction, *Something Happened,* may seem more probable than my own real-life account in showing how the will to believe can pervade a large organization. Few of the conditions that nurture the will to believe in Heller's world were factors at Maidenform. We had no spin doctors to foster belief in the infallibility of the company. Nor were we given to kidding ourselves or disguising reality on a routine basis. The will to believe was neither ingrained nor habitual. And this is just the point: Corporate self-deception can occur, as it did in the case of No-Show Naturals, under the most *im*probable of circumstances.

The Hidden Costs of the Will to Believe

In current American business practice, where efficiency is so highly prized, cost-*in*efficiencies may well seem the worst price to pay for the will to believe. Yet there are less tangible but equally damaging costs that can accrue from adhering to corporate gospel. While well-managed companies are usually resilient enough to absorb temporary financial losses, they can be hard put to disregard the human consequences—what I call the *hidden costs*—of a habitual will to believe. Executives tend to underestimate costs like these because they are hard to measure. It is part of Bob Slocum's fictional job description, on the other hand, to supply us with an antidote against chronic belief in corporate gospel by showing us what its hidden costs really are.

As we hear Bob Slocum out, we become aware that the will to believe carries with it certain damaging side effects. For Slocum, the chief by-product of his job of propagating good lies is a climate of fear. Fear, in fact, riddles the organization from top to bottom. And no wonder. In an environment where lies flourish and reality is stood on its head, insecurity, mistrust, and suspicion within the corporate hierarchy multiply accordingly. So much so, in fact, that this company has more than its share of nervous breakdowns and suicides. The prevailing corporate culture aggravates this condition precisely by avoiding the unwelcome idea that its employees might be unhappy. Slocum's words suggest that his company has been sanitized of unseemly displays of temperament:

> . . . we are encouraged to revolve around each other eight hours a day like self-lubricating ball bearings, careful not to jar or scrape. . . . (SH, 36)

Slocum's metaphor conveys a sense of the unreality of Heller's workplace. It is as though any recognizable human feeling has been siphoned off, leaving only preprogrammed responses. Heller's sardonic narrator finds an equally striking metaphor to dramatize the deadliness of enforced decorum:

> We come to work, have lunch, and go home. We goose-step in and goose-step out, change our partners and wander all about, sashay around for a pat on the head, and promenade home till we all drop dead. (SH, 26)

The main challenge for executives like Slocum has nothing to do with the actual business of the company (which somehow takes care of itself), but rather with neutralizing the fears to which the people they manage, those to whom they report, and they themselves are in thrall. Slocum and other executives who survive this atmosphere of corporate paranoia have their own special way of dealing with it. They embrace it. They absorb it into their systems, and Heller conveys this process by having Slocum speak in a dispassionate voice eerily devoid of any inflection or variation in tone:

> Most of us like working here, even though we are afraid, and do not long to leave for jobs with other companies. We make money and have fun. We read books and go to plays. And somehow the time passes. (SH, 18)

Slocum seems better adjusted than most because he harbors no illusions about what he himself does. Equally important, he understands how the corporate players relate to each other and to himself. A "color wheel," Slocum's ingenious organizational chart, allows him to trace these relationships sequentially and so stabilize a situation that threatens to spin out of control:

> So I scare Green, and Green scares White, and White scares Black, and Black scares Brown and Green, and Brown scares me. . . . (SH, 27)

Slocum proves as adept at feeding his superiors' illusions as at manufacturing lies. For example, he knows full well that the information provided by the sales force is useless because it is false, but he encourages the salesmen to submit their call reports anyway. Why? Simply because the senior executive in charge of sales and marketing, despite his knowing the reports are mostly lies, reminds Slocum that he has no more "reliable source of information on which to base his own decisions and reports. . . ." Slocum's own ability to tell *good* lies is the real source of his staying power. In reviewing his job performance, his superior warns him,

> "Don't lie to anyone around here unconvincingly, if you want to keep working for me." (SH, 47)

If Heller's cheerless comedy seems absurd, we need only look a little farther afield to the real world of commerce for proof of a collective will to believe that would grace the most far-fetched of fictions. I have in mind the way corporate America about every five years seizes on a supposedly new management "concept" or "approach" that holds out the promise of new life for stagnating companies, yet in fact bears striking resemblances to old ideas that have lived and died of natural causes. The most celebrated panacea of the 1990s, dubbed "reengineering" and touted as "revolutionary," shows how the fictions of business play out in real life.

Reengineering as Corporate Gospel

Five years ago a large number of American companies adopted as an article of faith a theory of management expounded by Michael Hammer and James Champy in their book, *Reengineering the Corporation.*[2] Its argument is that because customers have become more demanding, because competition has become fiercer and global in scale, and because the rate of change in business has accelerated, companies must streamline the overall processes by which they accomplish their work. Traditional hierarchical organizations and specialization of labor must be scrapped because they are incompatible with the goal of eliminating unnecessary work to save time and money and to service customers better.

Despite the authors' claims to the contrary, there is nothing in this overall goal that requires a "revolutionary" overhaul of operations. Corporate America has warmed to other concepts over the past quarter century that also entail resourcefulness in the use of labor, elimination of needless layers of management and redundant tasks, and concentration on customer needs. Among these are Management by Objectives, Total Quality Management, and Team-Based Management. The special fervor, however, with which so many top executives became true believers in reengineering, a concept that was to fail so many of them soon after they embraced it, is curious, but not surprising. In truth, reengineering was less a managerial concept addressing the genuine needs of most companies than a marketing ploy that deftly mined the rich vein of the corporate will to believe.

If timing is critical to marketing, then the timing of Hammer and Champy's purportedly new concept was exquisite. In general, "a time of great change," (to use Peter Drucker's description of the present) would seem to call for sweeping rather than incremental reforms. Reengineering urged precisely that, leaving no corner of the corporation untouched (or, better, unscathed). More specifically, reengineering provided a wonderfully convenient rationale for the rampant downsizing that so many American companies saw—and continue to see—as a prerequisite for survival in the 1990s. If you followed the dictates of the theory, such massive elimination of needless jobs was necessary to increase efficiency in customer service.

Truth to tell, most companies abhor change, especially the revolutionary changes in organizational structure advocated by the authors. Why should top management risk investing its resources to overhaul the organization for the sake of improvements that are hard to quantify before exhausting convenient short-term measures for generating profits and shareholder value? The fact of the matter is that *Reengineering the Corporation* met the need of chief executives for a concept weighty enough to legitimize—or, better, sanitize—the business of laying thousands of people off for reasons unrelated to reengineering. The title of the book itself, the attraction of which we should never underestimate, has a clarion ring to it, heralding a new age for floundering companies. There is nothing in it that is messy, that suggests the disruption of careers and erosion of traditional loyalties that have resulted from the layoffs over most of this decade. The chief virtue of reengineering for its fans was that it validated corporations' wholesale elimination of jobs in the name of a "revolution" that would allegedly make them more efficient and disciplined and so benefit those who survived. At the same time, it allowed cost-cutting executives to ignore the human costs involved, supposedly sacrificing the well-being of a few individuals in the interests of the long-term health of the organization.

A key principle of the will to believe, as we have already seen, is that you can disregard what is unpalatable—that is, you can ignore reality. In Bob Slocum's corporate life, one of the most absurd features is the company's ban on unhappiness. Lying, politicking, backbiting, paranoia, and sexual promiscuity are all tacitly sanctioned, but being unhappy is a cardinal sin in this fictitious corporate culture because it is abnormal. According to Slocum,

> The company takes a strong view against psychotherapy for executives because it denotes unhappiness, and unhappiness is a disgraceful social disease for which there is no excuse or forgiveness. Cancer, pernicious anemia, and diabetes are just fine, and even people with multiple sclerosis and Parkinson's disease may continue to go far in the company until they are no longer allowed to go on at all. But unhappiness is fatal. (SH, 500)

This effort to expunge unhappiness under the very conditions that create it is central to Heller's dark comedy. Yet the lines separating reality and fiction can and sometimes do become indistinct. In a series of investigative articles by *New York Times* reporters, later published in book form and entitled *The Downsizing of America*, the Chase bank was reported to have launched an aggressive campaign to shore up employee morale in the face of the fear, insecurity, and growing disillusionment caused by massive layoffs.[3] In the best tradition of participative management, Chase, according to the *Times*, invited all its employees to join in forging a new statement of values for the organization. These included teamwork, mutual respect, and professionalism, all duly inscribed on, among other places, coffee cups at the bank, so that, as the *Times* reporter put it, "every time you had some coffee, you drank the values, too." (DA, 43)

Not countenanced in this "feel-good" approach, apparently, was the possibility that anyone imbibing healthy values might be unhappy. One Chase manager who was interviewed mentioned that employees whose jobs were on the line were constantly surveyed to see how they felt. (The *Times* account reminds me of a visit to Disneyworld, where every so often a young, beaming employee pops up and asks, "Are you having a nice day?") For the bank manager and other employees with their jobs on the line, the question was not so innocuous, since bonuses and compensation were allegedly tied to the degree of declared employee satisfaction:

> "I would tell people, don't be stupid enough to say you were unhappy on that survey. But the truth is, we were unhappy. At one meeting the senior marketing guy screamed at us, 'I'm sick and tired of you guys complaining. If you're unhappy, leave.' We were shocked. We got yelled at for being unhappy. That made us even more unhappy." (DA, 44)

One can only hope that this Chase manager, like Bob Slocum, eventually understood that unhappiness can be "fatal" and accepted his plight. The will to believe, after all, is absolute: Because unhappiness was not an acceptable part of the new and improved statement of values, it didn't exist.

The boundary between fiction and reality is further blurred in the accounts by Heller and the *Times* of the pervasive paranoia consequent on the will to believe. In a scene that reads like a French farce, Heller shows how executives, driven alike by fear, fritter away their time jockeying for position, watching their backs, and contriving to know what is going on behind closed doors.

This scene happens early in the novel. Slocum is summoned to a meeting with Arthur Baron, a senior executive, who will tell him privately that the company's sales manager is to be fired and that he, Slocum, is in line to replace him. The scene functions, however, to show a series of knee-jerk reactions on the part of Kagle, the sales manager, and two other of Slocum's confreres, Green and Brown, all three of whom report to Baron and waylay Slocum on his way into and then out of the boss's office:

> Kagle pulls me to the side. 'What does he want?' he asks with alarm.
> 'How should I know?'
> 'Go see him.'
> 'What did you think I was going to do?'
> 'And come and tell me if he says anything about getting rid of me.' . . .
>
> 'Where are you going?' Green wants to know, as I pass him in the corridor on my way to [the boss's] office.
> 'Arthur Baron wants to see me.'
> Green skids to a stop with a horrified glare; and it's all I can do not to laugh in his face. . . .
>
> 'You come see me as soon as you've finished talking to him,' he orders.
> 'I want to know what he says. I want to know if I'm being fired or not.' . . .

'What did Arthur Baron want?' Johnny Brown asks.
'He wants me to put some jokes in a speech his son has to make at school.'
'You're . . . a liar.'
'A diplomat, Johnny.'
'But I'll find out.' (*SH*, 52,53,56,57)

The account of fearful bank executives in *The Downsizing of America* might well rival this one, were it not more pathetic than comic. In what the *Times* reporter, describing the situation at Chase, called a "Darwinian" struggle for survival, one manager reported seeing a colleague, also a close friend, chuckling in a conversation with their boss behind closed doors. "His first thought was that he was politicking. Could it be possible he was badmouthing him?" By tacit consent the two friends eventually stopped talking to each other. "Now they were both watching their backs," according to the report. (*DA*, 66–67) We can laugh at Heller's manic characters from a distance—until, of course, we find ourselves embroiled in the self-same predicament, or in a universe where these situations really do occur.

The sense of unreality that suffuses Bob Slocum's company is likewise evident in the ingenuity of beleaguered spokesmen forced to justify an increasingly desperate faith in the prevailing corporate gospel. In a 1995 *Wall Street Journal* interview with Hammer and Champy, the authors reverted to language reminiscent of Slocum's "ball bearing" metaphor and equally devoid of human associations. Asked whether consolidating jobs, so that one person performs the work of several, might not produce burnout, Hammer replied that "the individual is no longer a cog in the wheel; he is the wheel." Thus people find greater "fulfillment through their work." According to Hammer, the only problem with being "the wheel" (presumably as opposed to "big wheel") is that people "overdose on that"—as though the employees themselves were responsible for now having to work inhuman hours. Hammer's colorful term suggests a kind of hopeless addiction to work, for which workers have only themselves to blame. As for the "folks" in the middle (Hammer's friendly down-home term for loyal, long-term employees), they will now have to go because they are "hopelessly unqualified" to participate in the newly reengineered company.

For his part, Hammer's coauthor, Champy, placed the problem squarely on the shoulders of top management. Making a crucial distinction, he said, "Some of the companies are just downsizing and calling it reengineering. They haven't changed a damn thing." For Champy, apparently more mindful of the human implications than his associate, the "brutalization" of the workforce "has got to stop." And under what conditions will that take place? Why, when we "dramatically downsize and learn to do much more with much less."[4]

For the authors of *Reengineering the Corporation*, clichés, abstract metaphors, and double-talk betray the bankruptcy of their position. We might claim that taking refuge in generalizations, as Hammer and Champy did in the *Journal* interview, is harmless, were it not that their corporate acolytes have appeared to follow suit in justifying themselves.

A subsequent *Journal* article commented on how Digital Equipment's "dumbsizing" of its veteran sales force resulted in the loss of valued customers in Digital's health-industries group.[5] The director of health care at the company, defending his CEO's decision to make the drastic cuts, justified his boss's action by a novel use of a familiar metaphor:

> He had to make some quick decisions, and when you do that, you will throw part of the baby out with the bathwater. . . . He might have thrown out an arm and a leg, but he didn't throw out the whole body.

In other words, when you have to cut costs quickly, there will inevitably be some damage, but the organization will remain intact. We can only hope that the amputation at Digital was done with care, and the exposed limbs duly cauterized, whatever the time constraints may have been. The director's reliance on figurative language (as opposed, say, to a simple declarative statement) here proves a handy way to sustain the will to believe in the infallibility of corporate strategy.

The language of war and sports is especially useful for this purpose, since it is easy to relate to. According to the *Journal*, the same director at Digital, a propagandist surely worthy of Bob Slocum, acknowledged that the company failed to notify customers of its plans in a timely way, but insisted, "You can't afford to hit the customer one-on-one anymore." If companies can't "afford" to serve customers better, what *can* they afford? This is not so much a matter of doing "more with less" à la Champy, but of doing "less with

less," as the *Journal* rightly said. The will to believe invariably flies in the face of common sense.

The self-deception that accompanies obstinate adherence to company gospel took its most drastic and startling
form in Hammer's 1995 sequel, *The Reengineering Revolution*.[6] If anything, the new book represented a hardening of
Hammer's position on reengineering as a must in corporate
operations. If the reengineering revolution did not succeed
in most cases, the fault lay with the "counterrevolutionar-
ies" whose "mission" was to undermine reengineering. The
war metaphor was well chosen; it packed a real demagogic
punch. It is a familiar ploy of autocrats whose authority is
threatened. For Hammer, the critical mistake many companies made was not disposing of the "naysayers" early enough
in the game. Even more striking—and to my mind the
supreme instance of the will to believe—was Hammer's
denial of history itself:

> Claiming that we have said that reengineering has a 70
> percent failure rate, they [Hammer's critics] offer this sta-
> tistic as "proof" that reengineering doesn't work. How-
> ever, as we've stressed time and again, the reference they
> cite was a *historical observation, not a normative one* [italics
> mine]. While many companies *have* failed at reengineer-
> ing, no companies *need* fail. (*RR*, 171)

Of course they don't need to. But in the real world they
have failed. Evidently the only way for companies not to
have failed was to act in a "normative" way—that is, to do
exactly what the country's experts on reengineering told
them to do. In *The Reengineering Revolution*, as in all revolu-

tionary handbooks, categorical imperatives abound, reflecting the ossification of the will to believe:

> The failures failed because they did it wrong. Success is virtually guaranteed for those companies that go about reengineering with will, intelligence, and passion, and failure is similarly guaranteed for those that don't. (RR, 171)

The Denial of Reality and the Gospel of Shaw's Andrew Undershaft

Guarding against the tyranny of dogma such as that espoused by Hammer is never easy because simple answers to complex problems are immediately attractive. The fictions of business, I believe, provide an indispensable antidote to a rigid and simplistic mind-set, the bane of thoughtful executives. My favorite candidate for our present purposes is George Bernard Shaw's comedy, Major Barbara.[7] Written in 1906, the play is set in Edwardian England, a far remove from the brave new world of corporate reengineering, yet instructive in its treatment of those who, driven by the will to believe, would interpret reality according to their own lights.

On the face of it, Shaw, by his own admission a socialist, would be one of the least likely writers to offer sound advice to people making a living within a capitalistic system. We might well expect him to have little sympathy for a society built on capitalistic principles, let alone for capitalistic managers and leaders beset by the problem of the will to believe. There are any number of writers whose natural bias against the world of commerce dilutes whatever value as novels and plays their works might otherwise have. Good writers, however, are unpredictable and transcend facile categorizations. Shaw is one of them. In *Major Barbara*, the playwright tempers idealism with pragmatism, and conventional pieties with ruthless logic.

His play has all the trappings of an old-time melodrama. The heroine, Major Barbara, has joined the Salvation Army to minister to the poor as a saver of souls. In her person and in her works, Barbara has always repudiated her father, Andrew Undershaft, an immensely rich and powerful arms manufacturer. What Undershaft traffics in—namely, death and destruction—is abhorrent to her. *Major Barbara*, then, is ostensibly about a classic conflict of values: altruism and charity versus self-aggrandizement and greed.

The scenario of the play dramatizes this conflict in a straightforward way: Barbara and her father, both immensely strong in their convictions, agree to visit each other's bailiwick to test the strength of their respective beliefs. The passionately principled Barbara is convinced she can make a convert of her father, while he in his turn cautions that she may well disavow the Salvation Army "for the sake of the cannons."

A more sentimental or didactic playwright might well have chosen to cater to his audience and vindicate its conventional moral sense by showing how the hardened old capitalist is converted, despite himself, to the colors. Shaw, however, is one of those disagreeable writers with a fondness for confounding conventional expectations. In his hands the play takes quite another turn. Undershaft is endowed by his creator with a formidable intelligence that allows him to see through bias and pretension and thereby challenge the most cherished moral assumptions of his time.

The Gospel of Saint Andrew Undershaft, as Shaw puts it in his preface to the play, is that poverty is the greatest of man's evils rather than, as Saint Francis would have it, a "virtue to be embraced." Our first responsibility as citizens is "not to be poor." The fun of *Major Barbara*, of course, is not simply in Shaw's apparent heresy, but in his ability to embody this concept in comic dialogue and action.

In a scene at the Salvation Army shelter, before Undershaft appears, Shaw contrives to show that the purportedly firm spiritual foundations that sustain the Army are built on a thin fabric of self-deception. When Peter Shirley, an old down-and-outer represented as poor but honest, enters the shelter, weak from hunger, he refuses the meal that Jenny, a zealous young volunteer, sets before him, out of principle (as he likes to think):

> SHIRLEY: [*looking at it ravenously but not touching it, and crying like a child*] I never took anything before.
> JENNY: [*petting him*] Come, come! the Lord sends it to you: he wasn't above taking bread from his friends; and why should you be? Besides, when we find you a job you can pay us for it if you like.
> SHIRLEY: Yes, yes: that's true. I can pay you back: its only a loan. Oh Lord! oh Lord! [*He turns to the table and attacks the meal ravenously.*] (MB, 370)

The Salvation Army exists to save the souls of the poor, society's outcasts; the poor need the Salvation Army to eat and be saved, in that order. The veteran hangers-on, of course, play the game well because they know how to bolster the altruistic impulses of the people they rely on for their daily bread. As one of the faithful says, out of earshot, "Them Salvation lasses is dear good girls; but the better you are, the worse they likes to think you were before they rescued you."

Undershaft understands what drives the faithful all too well because he is a realist and harbors no illusions about himself:

BARBARA: By the way, papa, what is your religion?

UNDERSHAFT: My religion? Well, my dear, I am a Millionaire. That is my religion.

BARBARA: Then I'm afraid you and Mr. Shirley won't be able to comfort one another after all. You're not a Millionaire, are you Peter?

SHIRLEY: No; and proud of it.

UNDERSHAFT: [gravely] Poverty, my friend, is not a thing to be proud of.

SHIRLEY: [angrily] Who made your millions for you? Me and my like. What's kep us poor? Keepin you rich. I wouldn't have your conscience, not for all your income.

UNDERSHAFT: I wouldn't have your income, not for all your conscience, Mr. Shirley. (MB, 380)

To his credit, Andrew Undershaft also understands what currently drives the Salvation Army, or at least this particular shelter—namely, the funding that he personally provides from his purportedly immoral trade. He wins his joust with his daughter—"buying" the Salvation Army in effect—

when he offers to subsidize an operation increasingly desperate for money. A Mrs. Baines, who is cast as the Salvation Army Commissioner, discovers within herself an ingenious justification for accepting with a clear conscience what Barbara sees as blood money: "Dear Barbara. . . . If heaven has found a good way to make use of his money, are we to set ourselves up against the answer to our prayers?" The path to righteousness, it would seem, is facilitated by healthy rationalization, a particularly virulent form of the will to believe.

The gospel of Andrew Undershaft is nowhere better vindicated than in the verbal jousting between him and a character Shaw invents as his intellectual peer. Adolphus Cusins, a professor of Greek, has fallen in love with Barbara and has joined the Salvation Army strictly on her account, not, as it turns out, because he believes in the Salvation Army. He, like Undershaft, perceives the weakness of its assumptions about its operation; and to that extent, the two understand one another. Nonetheless, there is a fundamental difference between them. Cusins is a moralist, and the sharpest dialogue in the play consists of Undershaft's increasingly effective efforts to win the young man over to *his* religion (money). Claiming smugly to be "a sort of collector of religions," Cusins rather patronizingly asks Undershaft whether there is anything "out of the common" about *his* religion:

UNDERSHAFT: Only that there are two things necessary to Salvation.

CUSINS: [*disappointed, but polite*] Ah, the Church Catechism. . . .

UNDERSHAFT: The two things are—

CUSINS: Baptism and—

UNDERSHAFT: No. Money and gunpowder.

CUSINS: [*surprised, but interested*] That is the general opinion of our governing classes. The novelty is in hearing any man confess it.

UNDERSHAFT: Just so.

CUSINS: Excuse me: is there any place in your religion for honor, justice, truth, love, mercy and so forth?

UNDERSHAFT: Yes: they are the graces and luxuries of a rich, strong, and safe life.

CUSINS: Suppose one is forced to choose between them and money or gunpowder?

UNDERSHAFT: Choose money and gunpowder; for without enough of both you cannot afford the others. (MB, 384–385)

The climactic scene in *Major Barbara*, again between Undershaft and Cusins, recalls Michael Hammer's efforts to sustain his will to believe in reengineering when that "revolutionary" concept faltered in many of its real-life applications. The philosophical revolutionary, Cusins, believes that society can be reformed by peaceful and democratic means. The realist, Undershaft, insists that his armaments alone provide the "only real lever strong enough to overturn a social system":

UNDERSHAFT: When you vote, you only change the names of the cabinet. When you shoot, you pull down governments, inaugurate new epochs, abolish old orders and set up new. Is that historically true, Mr. Learned Man, or is it not?

CUSINS: It is historically true. I loathe having to admit it. I repudiate your sentiments. I abhor your nature. I defy you in every possible way. Still, it is true. But it ought not to be true.

UNDERSHAFT: Ought! ought! ought! ought! ought! Are you going to spend your life saying ought, like the rest of our moralists? Turn your thoughts into shalls, man. Come and make explosives with me. Whatever can blow men up can blow society up. The history of the world is the history of those who can embrace this truth. (MB, 436)

Cusins cannot have it both ways; he cannot occupy his moral high ground and, at the same time, deny the truth of history. In finally renouncing his will to believe in the immorality of arms manufacturers, Shaw's philosopher becomes a munitions maker.

I suspect that Shaw, were he alive, would denounce the will to believe as an evil second only to poverty itself. At the very least, I believe that he would not pull his punches with Michael Hammer if the latter stubbornly clung to what *need* not be true, just as Shaw's Cusins hangs on to what "*ought* not to be true.*" Certainly the will to believe is most pernicious where it conflicts with entrenched beliefs, and Shaw is astute enough to know that it can afflict the brightest people. In language stripped of cant and pretense, he loosens our grip on the fictions we cling to by showing us the realities we avoid.

I believe that an organization really looking after its best interests can take the cue from Shaw and minimize its dependence on traditional formulas and conventional beliefs. The playwright has shown us that what we take most for granted is often baseless. The way Maidenform came to repudiate some of the time-honored tenets of advertising in building a national brand is a modern example of this principle.

Because consumer research has always shown that superior fit and comfort are the most important features in a bra, it would appear to be self-evident that the most effective advertising would allow women to see clearly how a bra fits and what it looks like on the body. In planning its landmark advertising campaign for 1949 with the company's agency, Norman, Craig, and Kummel, Maidenform began with a more fundamental premise: that women are more than a sum total of individual body parts and that an appeal to their self-esteem by way of making them feel good about themselves might have a powerful effect. Maidenform's Dream campaign broke new ground by capturing the feelings of women in the postwar era. For the millions of women who, having contributed to the war effort on the home front, were once again encouraged to return to the traditional, dependent, and contingent roles of wife and mother, daughter and girlfriend, the new Dream campaign fed their need for romance, independence, and personal achievement through a series of wish-fulfillment fantasies in which they played starring roles ("I dreamed I barged down the Nile in my Maidenform bra"; "I dreamed I swayed the jury in my Maidenform bra"). This new creative approach caused an immediate sensation on radio and in print, where parodies quickly assured Maidenform's Dream campaign a place in American popular culture. By any standard, the Dream ads were among the most successful in the history of advertising.

A series of TV and print ads that Maidenform and the agency Levine, Huntley, Schmidt, & Beaver developed in the late 1980s pursued the emotional appeal of the Dream campaign, but took the idea one leap further. By freeing ourselves from the conventional constraints of having to portray a bra on a body, regardless of the setting or situation, we opened up new creative approaches to advertising lingerie, reflecting the sensibilities of the truly liberated woman. A series of commercials featured male celebrities like Omar Sharif, Pierce Brosnan, Michael York, and Corbin Bernsen talking about *their* fantasies of women who wear flattering lingerie:

> Lingerie says a lot about a woman. I listen as often as possible. Lingerie doesn't cover a woman's body so much as uncover her personality. It tells me how she feels about herself. It also tells me how she feels about me . . . if I get to see it. (Michael York, 1988 ad)

In a subsequent TV commercial set to a chorus of children's voices singing, "Did you ever see a lassie go this way and that?" a series of shots of women's bodices strapped and corseted in unnatural-looking costumes from centuries past was followed by the line, "Isn't it nice to live in a time when women aren't being pushed around so much anymore?" Still another Maidenform TV commercial depicted a series of comic stereotypes of women ranging from sex kitten and battle-ax to rich matron, ending with the line, "While these images of women are simple and obvious, women themselves rarely are. Just something we like to keep in mind when designing our lingerie."

These ads and TV commercials indeed struck a chord with our customers. Many consumers wrote to us directly, emphasizing how "disgruntled" they were "at seeing graphically depicted women's underwear staring out from buses, transit shelters, magazines, and newspapers," and how, on the other hand, the Maidenform ads showed "respect for the female sex" and for "our value as people." What matters for our purposes here is that, once we had thus shifted the conceptual framework of our advertising, with possibilities for the creative team now apparently unlimited, our old *assumption* about the need to display merchandise on a model in a lingerie ad automatically became untenable. To have persisted in our will to believe in an advertising doctrine that may (or may not) have been appropriate to another day would have been to limit our ability to develop a unique consumer franchise for the Maidenform brand.

As Shaw's unconventional arms manufacturer well knew, new ideas that often seem outrageous turn out, when aired, to be based on common sense. We had jettisoned traditional beliefs about intimate apparel advertising and positioned Maidenform not simply as a manufacturer of bras, but as a company that truly understands women. Did that approach not continue to reflect the real nature of our business: making women feel good about themselves? And could it not be said that the basic function of consumer advertising in our case was not so much to sell a best-selling style as to predispose women to buy the Maidenform brand, whatever their choice of styles among a bewildering selection on the selling floor might be?

How we think about issues and values in business is more important, in my view, than *what* we think about them. To compartmentalize our thinking, to reduce it to a single frame of reference, is to "fall victim to our own propaganda," to use Bob Slocum's phrase. I sometimes wonder how Shaw, were he to enjoy reincarnation as a management consultant, might comment on some of the common assumptions about management and leadership in our own time.

For one thing, Shaw would be certain to decry the popular notion that today, when traditional loyalties to our firms are eroding, "team players" are a leader's most valued asset. For him "team player" would undoubtedly mean a person within an organization who is malleable, who conforms to the company culture, and who never challenges the status quo. Nonteam players, I hear him insisting, are more valuable to a vital organization. Nonteam players show their independence by their willingness to question corporate gospel and to take nothing for granted. This doesn't mean that their loyalty to the company is suspect. On the contrary, they show their loyalty by speaking their minds—indeed, by being outspoken on critical matters and marshaling facts without distorting them. They do *not* conform to the prevailing company culture, nor should they be expected to; their value lies precisely in *challenging* it, in operating outside the pale. The company willing to act on their recommendations will benefit precisely because their proposals flout conventional wisdom. (My new consultant, Shaw, allergic as he is to catchphrases, would surely remind us that "conventional wisdom" is an oxymoron, and that, curiously, we seldom hear about "unconventional wisdom," as though it were a contradiction in terms.)

As a pragmatist, how would Shaw advise CEOs to go about solving the knotty problem of encouraging unconventional thinking on the part of managers protective of their jobs in their newly reengineered companies? Knowing executives' predilection for sports analogies and his own penchant for standing familiar orthodoxies on their heads, Shaw might well tell them about Walter Hagen. Hagen was one of the great golfers of the 1930s. He often said that he owed his success not to his ability to play consistent error-free golf, but to his conviction that he was bound to make a certain number of mistakes even in the best of rounds. By actually *planning* on making a given number of mistakes before he set out, Hagen could forget about a bad shot or two, whereas lesser golfers, as he well knew, would usually let a patch of ragged golf discompose them and ruin the rest of their rounds. As usual, Shaw's recommendation to the corporate hierarchy seems shocking until, on reflection, we see that it makes sense. Business leaders bent on stimulating "out-of-the-box" thinking that goes against the corporate grain might do well to establish their own mistake-quota, wherein everyone is permitted to make a certain number of errors with impunity—provided, we might add, that they are not thoughtless errors.

And what would Shaw have to say about corporate leadership in today's ultracompetitive environment? Most assuredly he would *not* agree with Michael Hammer that it is time to get rid of the naysayers and to close ranks. More than ever, I hear him saying, we need to test our own most closely held convictions rather than to try to convince each other of their validity. More than ever we need to create a corporate environment where people understand that it is not simply their prerogative but their *responsibility* to scrutinize the collective wisdom. Only then will we have the opportunity to avoid situations where, despite ourselves, wishes become beliefs; and beliefs, before long, are accepted as gospel truth.

5

SURVIVAL OF THE FITTEST IN A DARWINIAN BUSINESS WORLD

He believed in the financial rightness of the thing he had done. He was entitled to do it. Life was war—particularly financial life; and strategy was its keynote, its duty, its necessity. Why should he bother about petty, picayune minds which could not understand this?

Theodore Dreiser, *The Financier*

It would be easy, I think, to measure what it will take to succeed in business in the twenty-first century by reference to a term from the nineteenth: "survival of the fittest." Charles Darwin used this phrase to describe the evolutionary process of "natural selection" in the animal world. In the *Origin of Species* (1859), Darwin maintained that those creatures who adapted to changes in the environment were bound to prevail, while those who could not were doomed to extinction. If we substitute "companies" for "creatures," we would have a description of the current business climate as well.

For American empire builders like John D. Rockefeller, Darwin's law of nature was no different from the law of the marketplace. "The growth of a large business," he once remarked, was "merely a survival of the fittest." Rockefeller knew whereof he spoke. In building his megalith, Standard Oil, he threatened to crush his competitors if they refused to sell out to him. Very few did—refuse, that is. Andrew Carnegie was Rockefeller's match in phrasemaking as well as empire building. The "law of competition," he proclaimed, while sometimes "hard for the individual," was "best for the race," since it ensured "the survival of the fittest in every department." Thus did these titans of commerce validate their claims to power and wealth.

Today, a laissez-faire economy, fierce global competition for key markets, massive restructuring in the interests of greater efficiency, and shareholders' demands for sustained quarterly profits signal the resurgence of a survival-of-the-fittest business culture. Bulking up is as requisite to survival in our time as it was in Rockefeller's. Take the unprecedented number of government-sanctioned mergers and acquisitions in global industries. In covering Boeing's $14 billion acquisition of McDonnell Douglas in 1997, the *New York Times* emphasized "efficiency, cost-cutting and exports—in other words, commercial success in a Darwinian marketplace."[1]

Nor can it be any surprise that today's exemplary empire builder, Bill Gates, has been characterized by a former Microsoft executive thus:

> He's Darwinian. He doesn't look for win-win situations with others, but for ways to make others lose. Success is defined as flattening the competition. . . .[2]

That Gates knows how to exploit a competitive advantage is indisputable, and it stamps him as a true Darwinian. "The slightest *advantage* in one [species] . . . over those with which it comes into *competition* . . . will turn the balance," Darwin had concluded.

On all corporate levels, the efficiencies presumably gained through a combination of acquisitions and downsizing means that managers and their employees are working harder than ever to maintain the same standard of living, let alone keep their jobs. "Darwin's Delight" is the way the *Wall Street Journal* described the plight of seven vice presidents of First Interstate Bancorp whose jobs were on the line after Wells Fargo's 1996 takeover of their bank. The atmosphere at First Interstate was a "macabre lottery, rife with speculation over whether anyone will survive." Technological advances have increased the pressure to "adapt or lose out," as another news report recently put it. Despite the lowest level of unemployment in decades, "many [adults] sense they are trapped in a Darwinian struggle, with the computer literate atop the food chain."[3]

Notwithstanding the hardship that Carnegie saw as inevitable for some in the Darwinian "struggle for existence," American business prosperity would seem to vindicate a survival-of-the-fittest business culture. Perhaps. I maintain, though, that in flush times it behooves us to be self-critical rather than self-congratulatory. The fictions of business remind us of values that are distinctively human at a time when, as business managers, we are most apt to be overzealous in the pursuit of self-interest and efficiency.

Implicit in the fictions of business pertinent to the current resurgence of Darwinism is an examination of the values—the ideas, principles, and attitudes—that affect the way we do business and treat the people with whom we work. What does the pursuit of self-interest actually entail? How does it affect other people, and does this really matter? When and under what conditions does the pursuit of self-interest become counterproductive? Similarly, when does our pursuit of efficiencies in business in the interest of greater profitability and productivity become self-defeating? Does it matter whether we view efficiency as an end in itself rather than as a means to an end? By raising these and like questions, the fictions of business keep us thinking about what we value as people, not simply as business-people.

None of the fictions I have in mind are contemporary—they were published from 1906 to 1937—but all have continuing relevance to our time in showing us how an addiction to self-interest and efficiency can permeate our culture and what its consequences are likely to be. Theodore Dreiser's *The Financier* is the story of a streetcar magnate whose rise to wealth and power challenges our conventional assumptions about ambition and the uses of power. Sinclair Lewis's *Babbitt* is the story of a conventional man whose mindless adherence to the gospel of efficiency strips him of any independence or individuality he might otherwise have had. John Dos Passos's *The Big Money* and Upton Sinclair's *The Jungle* are about the dehumanizing effects on rank-and-file workers of the struggle for survival in an age of mechanization. Despite changing times, the human issues and conflicts implicit in these fictions continue to command our attention.

The Financier: Theodore Dreiser's Darwinian Businessman

Theodore Dreiser's novel, *The Financier,* appeared in 1912 after being rejected by a number of publishing houses for being uncompromising in its realism.[4] I suspect that many would think it so in our day as well. Dreiser's central character, Frank Cowperwood, is a financial wizard who, despite his contempt for time-honored social and ethical standards, even the law itself, elicits the reader's admiration. *The Financier,* set in the late nineteenth century, recounts how Cowperwood, the son of a Philadelphia banker, achieves power and wealth through a combination of innovative financial maneuvering, a will powerful enough to make influential people do his bidding, extraordinary personal charm, and an indifference to anyone but himself.

As a realist, Dreiser recorded life as he saw it. He had no morals to preach and no interest in pandering to popular tastes by sidestepping harsh facts. Unlike the Horatio Alger books, in which a shoeshine boy rises to respectability in nineteenth-century America by displaying the requisite moral virtues of selflessness and hard work, *The Financier* depicts its central character hard at work in the single-minded pursuit of his own self-interest. "I satisfy myself" is Cowperwood's credo; and Dreiser goes on to comment that it "might well have been emblazoned upon any coat of arms which he could have contrived to set forth his claim to intellectual and social nobility."

Conventional novels—which is to say most novels— before and after Dreiser's time typically depict aggressive, egocentric businesspeople like Cowperwood as rising in the world only to be upended by their own self-delusion or the envy of others. The rise and fall of the mighty is a story-telling theme that can be traced as far back as the medieval morality play. Dreiser's scenario is a rare and riveting exception. *The Financier* relates how Frank Cowperwood, lusting after power and wealth, attains those ends, falls, and then rises again, unchastened and newly empowered, in a better position than ever to fulfill his ambitions.

As early as the age of ten, Dreiser's Darwinian hero reaches what will become his life-long conviction that the only operative law in the universe is the law of nature. To make his point, Dreiser tells the story of a struggle for survival between a lobster and a squid, as the young Frank Cowperwood sees and understands it.

One day the boy passes by a fish market near his house where he spots a tank on display in which a lobster and a squid have been placed. The lobster, it seems, has been given no food because the squid "was considered his rightful prey." The two creatures play a cat-and-mouse game, in which the lobster sits on the bottom of the tank with his "beady, black buttons of eyes" never off the squid. The latter moves about "in torpedo fashion." But the lobster is relentless in tracking his prey's movements. Little by little, pieces of the squid's body begin to disappear.

> The lobster would leap like a catapult to where the squid was apparently idly dreaming, and the squid, very alert, would dart away, shooting out at the same time a cloud of ink, behind which it would disappear. It was not always completely successful, however. Small portions of its

body or its tail were frequently left in the claws of the monster below. (F, 8)

Cowperwood is fascinated by this struggle. One morning, "his nose almost pressed to the glass," he sees that only "a portion of the squid remained." It is only a matter of time now. Sure enough, that same evening he sees a little crowd gathered in front of the tank. The squid, exhausted from his efforts, can no longer elude the lobster. Having learned to anticipate the squid's movements, the lobster has seized it in its claws, severed its body, and partially devoured it.

The inevitability of this deadly drama is not lost on the thoughtful young Cowperwood: "The squid couldn't kill the lobster—he had no weapon. The lobster could kill the squid—he was heavily armed." For the boy, the incident is a paradigm of life itself. The world is a natural hierarchy of predators and their victims, the strong and the weak. Just as lobsters live on squid, so men live on lobsters. Finally, at the top of the chain, who lives on men? Why, "other men," Cowperwood concludes after some deliberation. *The Financier* is the story of how Frank Cowperwood, in his lust for power, reenacts the drama of the lobster and the squid, always mindful of the laws of nature in the world of men.

Like a true Darwinian, Dreiser's Cowperwood demonstrates early in his career that he possesses the instincts for survival in a predatory world:

A real man—a financier—was never a tool. He used tools. He created. He led. . . . Clearly, very clearly, at nineteen, twenty, and twenty-one years of age, he saw all this. . . . (F, 42)

Cowperwood's long-term goal is to leverage his power and resources as a financier to buy up the controlling shares of Philadelphia's streetcar system, increasingly vital to a post–Civil War economic boom. In this enterprise, he has several things going for him. There is, first of all, his financial acumen. Cowperwood's chief method is to orchestrate the money he borrows to finance his purchases of streetcar stock, paying off each loan as it comes due with other borrowed funds. At the same time, he proves adroit in influencing the prices of streetcar stock in innovative ways that border on the unethical, but that work to his advantage. Dreiser's metaphor for Cowperwood's machinations lends an almost aesthetic quality to a natural predator:

> Like a spider in a spangled net, every thread of which he knew, had laid, had tested, he [Cowperwood] had surrounded and entangled himself in a splendid, glittering network of connections, and he was watching all the details. (F, 140)

Equally important to his string of successes is Cowperwood's ability to project an inner confidence and strength of mind. This is an individual whom people know they can trust to invest their money safely and wisely. Most significant of all, however, is the financier's instinct for seeking out and exploiting those individuals who, he calculates, might best serve his ends.

> He was concerned to see only what was of vast advantage to him, and to devote all his attention to that. (F, 78)

His big opportunity in this regard soon comes.

As his reputation as a financier grows, Cowperwood draws the attention of Philadelphia's political movers and shakers. These are men who think nothing of using their positions of power to line their own pockets. In their world, the lack of real financial regulations at the time allows them to make interest-free "loans" from city and state tax funds, to invest the money, and to return only the principal to the city treasury after pocketing the interest. These politicians see Cowperwood as a man who can invest large amounts of public funds for them at substantial rates of interest. Of course, they make it clear that he will get his own share of the spoils.

Cowperwood is ever the pragmatist. While he appears to have been drawn into tacit collusion with the most powerful men in the state, Dreiser makes it clear that his financier is, in reality, using *them* to further his own plan to control the streetcar lines. Cowperwood knows that, in addition to earning his commission, he can invest the politicians' "loans" at a higher rate of interest than what he has guaranteed them and pocket the difference.

More valuable still for his purposes is the acquaintance he strikes up with the city treasurer, an insignificant bureaucrat called Stener. Cowperwood is quick to realize that this individual is of "considerable importance for the simple reason that he was weak." Unbeknownst to the politicians, Cowperwood convinces Stener to rubber-stamp a loan from the treasury by promising to share the proceeds of the invested funds with him alone. The source of Cowperwood's strength lies in knowing that he can best serve his own interests by exploiting the self-interest of others.

In presenting such a character as sympathetic, Dreiser is less cynical than he is realistic. He is simply asking what it takes to prevail in a society in which self-interest is the norm.

> . . . Cowperwood was an opportunist. And by this time his financial morality had become special and local in its character. There were so many situations wherein what one might do in the way of taking or profiting was open to discussion and doubt. Morality varied, in his mind at least, with conditions. . . . Here, in Philadelphia, the tradition was that the city treasurer might use the money of the city without interest so long as he returned the principal intact. The city treasury and the city treasurer were like a honey-laden hive and a queen bee around which the drones—the politicians—swarmed in the hope of profit. (F, 133–134)

For Dreiser, Cowperwood's singular lack of illusions makes him a model capitalist. The man who best succeeds in leveraging his power in a predatory environment will prevail. From the financier's vantage point,

> . . . it was so very evident, in so many ways, that force was the answer—great mental and physical force. Why these giants of commerce and money could do as they pleased in this life, and did. (F, 121)

Dreiser, of course, is also realistic enough to know that fate often has the upper hand in the affairs of men—even the strongest, who "live on other men." So well equipped is

Cowperwood to deal with the world as it is that only an act of God, we suppose, can thwart him. In fact, that is exactly what happens.

The great Chicago fire of 1871, decimating the financial center of that city, sends the financial markets around the country into a tailspin. Panic causes everyone from whom Cowperwood has borrowed money to finance his purchases of streetcar stock to call in their loans at the same time. The financier has relied largely on the old strategy of "borrowing from Peter to pay Paul," and the value of the stocks that he owns has plummeted. Desperate for quick additional funding, Cowperwood appeals to his erstwhile ally, Stener, to advance him $60,000 to cover his immediate losses. The city treasurer, afraid of any further secret dealings with the exposed Cowperwood, refuses him. In desperation, the financier secretly prevails on Stener's unwitting assistant to sign off on the $60,000 without his boss's consent. Though the sum is paltry compared to the hundreds of thousands he has borrowed and repaid in collusion with Stener, this time Cowperwood is found out and tried in court.

Characteristically, Cowperwood is unrepentant and unbowed. In fact, Dreiser gives us the impression that he is in as much control of the situation as ever. "These lawyers, this jury, this straw-and-water judge, these machinations of fate, did not basically disturb or humble or weaken him." In Frank Cowperwood's universe, the law of nature prevails over the law of man. To the strong belong the spoils.

He believed in the financial *rightness* of the things he had done. He was entitled to do it. Life was war—particularly financial life; and strategy was its keynote, its duty, its necessity. Why should he bother about petty, picayune minds which could not understand this? (*F*, 306)

One of the most telling ironies of Dreiser's novel is that the very people who convict Cowperwood are shown to be in accord with the financier's Darwinian view of life. The prosecuting attorney, a man named Shannon, is vociferous in his condemnation of Cowperwood in front of the jury ("this defendant has one of the most subtle and dangerous minds of the criminal financier type"). Yet Dreiser is careful to distinguish between the public prosecutor and the private man whose self-interest is at one with the man he seeks to convict:

> As between man and man, Shannon was not particularly opposed to the case Steger [Cowperwood's lawyer] had made out for Cowperwood, nor was he opposed to Cowperwood's having made money as he did. As a matter of fact, Shannon actually thought that if he had been in Cowperwood's position, he would have done exactly the same thing. However, he was the newly elected district attorney. He had a record to make. . . .(*F*, 315)

What's more, Shannon is beholden to the political forces of the city that are using Cowperwood as their scapegoat, lest their own financial transgressions, so many of which have involved Cowperwood, come to light. As far as they are concerned, Cowperwood must be convicted, not because in their eyes he has done anything wrong, but only "for the looks of the thing."

By implication, the members of the jury—architect and grocer, manufacturer and florist, contractor and merchant—

also share Cowperwood's view that the laws of nature take precedence over the laws of men. Most believe him to be guilty, but not because of moral indignation at Cowperwood's purported criminality. Quite the contrary, they waver because they are uncertain of the grounds for convicting him, legal arguments notwithstanding. The truth is that they have to convict him only because, *technically* speaking, he happened to get caught taking something that was not his. Cowperwood thus embodies, albeit in exaggerated form, the aspirations of society as a whole. If, indeed, success in business depends on the survival of the fittest, then who would not want to emulate Frank Cowperwood?

That Theodore Dreiser's financier, far from being broken by a prison term, emerges unshaken to launch his career anew is altogether consistent with what we know about Cowperwood's resolve and extraordinary abilities. Dreiser, like his hero, looks at life unflinchingly. In so doing, he convinces us that the businessperson who combines genius with great daring and force can be neither constrained nor judged by conventional rules, regulations, or moral norms. I find it impossible to forget Dreiser's Darwinian hero in reading contemporary nonfiction accounts of the career and criminal trial of a latter-day Cowperwood, Michael Milken.

Theodore Dreiser, Meet Michael Milken

I am struck by how closely fact sometimes replicates fiction, or, put another way, how life imitates art. The account of the financial intrigues of Michael Milken and his Wall Street associates in the eighties by James B. Stewart, formerly the front-page editor of *The Wall Street Journal,* brought home to me the marked similarities between Milken's career and that of Cowperwood.[5] Given the way Cowperwood's credo, "I satisfy myself," could just as well apply to Milken, I should draw a direct line from the late-nineteenth- to the late-twentieth-century financier. Overall, both men built on their experiences as traders in brokerage houses to construct personal financial empires. Each achieved his ends using financial techniques so innovative and sophisticated for their time that few could fully understand them, let alone question their legitimacy. Each was a pioneer in the world of finance.

In his *Den of Thieves,* which appeared in 1991 and became the number one nonfiction best-seller, Stewart highlights the key element that contributed to the fabulous success of Milken (and, as it happens, of Cowperwood): the exceptional freedom he enjoyed in using his financial resources to build an empire. According to Stewart, Milken's advocacy of high-yield or "junk" bonds as a way of financing new ventures was scorned at first by the Wall Street investment community because of the high degree of risk they carried. Despite the risk, the market for these bonds was "almost entirely unregulated" in the late 1970s. Milken was able to charge enormous commissions and fees, Stewart points out, because there was no published listing of the prices of his offerings. The author's description of Milken's financial monopoly at this time recalls the survival-of-the-fittest culture in which Dreiser's Cowperwood flourished:

> The world of junk bonds was the financial equivalent of
> the early days of the American frontier; a rough justice
> was extracted from the *weak* by the *strong.*" (*DT,* 47)

For Milken, as for Cowperwood, the accumulation of wealth was not an end in itself. As *Den of Thieves* demonstrates, the goal for both was power—the power that financial strength made possible. Just as Cowperwood used his financial acumen for the purpose of buying up and eventually monopolizing the streetcar lines in Philadelphia, so Milken was quick to realize that his junk-bond offerings could be a potent weapon in what came to be known as the leveraged buyout. As Stewart succinctly puts it, "With corporate control went power."

The leveraging of political power to further their ends was integral to the strategy of both Milken and Cowperwood. Stewart suggests that the tacit collusion of influential politicians in Milken's financial activities was assured by Drexel Burnham's contributions to Political Action Committees during Milken's tenure there. Cowperwood's ability to make handsome returns on the Philadelphia politicians' investments bespeaks a more direct collaboration, but it similarly ensures a laissez-faire attitude toward the world of finance.

In adversity as in prosperity, Milken and Cowperwood are almost the mirror image of each other. Just as the financial panic of the 1870s was the undoing of Cowperwood, so the market crash of 1987 occasioned the unraveling of Milken's "junk bond" empire. Each was tried and found guilty of mishandling his client's money, and each was jailed for between one and two years. Characteristic of both financiers was their unwavering belief in the legitimacy of their financial operations and, at the same time, in the arbitrariness of the legal system pitted against them. "The force in this country buying high-yield securities has overpowered all regulation," Milken told the *Washington Post*, echoing Cowperwood's faith in the "financial *rightness* of the thing he had done."

Both rebounded from their prison terms unscathed and unchastened. Just as Cowperwood stood poised at the end of his prison term to resuscitate his plans to become a streetcar magnate, so Milken (to update Stewart's account) quickly reestablished himself as a recognized financial guru. The junk-bond market that he created in the 1970s and for which he was subsequently scorned and discredited is once again making possible many of the corporate consolidations of the late 1990s. That J. P. Morgan, among other white-shoe firms, is underwriting these bonds lends them a greater legitimacy than ever.

I have a feeling that Theodore Dreiser, were we to beam him up to us, would be intrigued by this saga of self-interest operating in a world of resurgent Darwinism. The strong parallels in the lives and times of the two financiers would not escape him. I am sure, too, that the virulent, polarized debate on Milken's character and culpability would be grist for his mill.

The rise, fall, and phoenix-like recovery of Michael Milken follows the plot of *The Financier* and, I believe, provides a real-life vindication of Dreiser's view that, in a society in which the pursuit of self-interest is pervasive, the cunning, force, and daring characteristic of the "fittest" will carry the day and challenge conventional thinking and ethical considerations. That Dreiser's view is not a popular one is evident today in the anti-Milken tracts, which by my count, outweigh the pro-Milken advocates by about five to one. *Den of Thieves*, the most influential of the anti-Milken tracts, makes its appeal to popular prejudice by wedding its unqualified condemnation of Milken's financial methods to incendiary rhetoric.

As the title and epigraph of his book imply, Stewart sees Milken as the embodiment of moral turpitude. He borrows "den of thieves" from Matthew 21: 12-13, where Jesus banishes the moneychangers from the temple, declaring: "My house shall be called the house of prayer; but ye have made it a den of thieves." The two parts of Stewart's book, called "Above the Law" and "The Chase," respectively, have the quality of a true-life suspense novel, with Milken and his crowd finding ingenious ways to make tons of money and evade the "feds" (part one), who slowly but inevitably close in on them (part two). There can be no mistaking who the villains and heroes are in this scenario. Milken was at the center of the "greatest criminal conspiracy the financial world has ever known," attempting to thwart the "heroic efforts of underpaid, overworked government lawyers."

Less strident and more convincing, I find, is Daniel Fischel's 1995 book, *Payback: The Conspiracy to Destroy Michael Milken and His Financial Revolution.*[6] As his own title implies, Fischel, a professor of law at the University of Chicago, sees Milken as revolutionary in the techniques he developed for financing businesses. Like many revolutionaries, Milken was easily made a scapegoat. Fischel insists that the financier was the untimely victim of a public outcry against the so-called decade of greed. For Fischel, this phrase was typical of the acrimonious rhetoric that played to people's prejudices. Further, it was rhetoric

purportedly fanned by a government anxious to find someone to prosecute to avoid responsibility for the savings and
loan disasters of the 1980s. Stewart, according to Fischel,
was simply the journalistic "mouthpiece" for government
prosecutors.

Aside from his belief that Milken was victimized, Fischel maintains that if it were not for Milken's innovative
methods of financing, many new businesses would not have
got off the ground. Similarly, the use of junk bonds to facili-
tate "the much maligned wave of hostile takeovers and
leveraged buyouts" was good for business generally, since
combining two firms "may create economies or efficiencies,
in which case the whole is greater than the parts." Restruc-
tured firms, according to the author, were "typically leaner
and more profitable operations as a result," thus ensuring
themselves a competitive advantage in the global economy
of the late twentieth century.

Fischel does not ignore the fact that Milken was tried
and found guilty by a federal judge. Yet he maintains that
what Stewart calls a "criminal conspiracy" has no basis in
fact, and that prosecutors could not prove that any of the
crimes Milken was charged with actually occurred. In
short, Fischel views Milken as Milken continues to view
himself—a financial visionary "who should be viewed as
the ultimate personification of the American dream."
That the use of junk bonds in subsidizing new businesses is
now standard practice in the late 1990s demonstrates how
the true visionary, fully armed with the courage and daring
to pursue his vision, can prevail in a world where only the
fittest survive.

The Tyranny of Efficiency

Like self-interest, efficiency is a watchword for a Darwinian business world. If we take efficiency to mean the allocation of our resources in the most productive manner, then it would certainly be difficult to underestimate its importance. Without efficient operations to sustain profitable growth and a competitive advantage, even today's most well-established businesses will founder. And after all, who can argue with success? Isn't increased efficiency in both manufacturing and service industries one of the top reasons for a burgeoning economy and American dominance in several worldwide markets in the late 1990s?

That said, I also maintain that the overzealous pursuit of efficiency as a corporate imperative can undermine the long-term interests of a company. Perhaps not since American industry embraced Frederick Taylor's time/study methods at the beginning of this century has efficiency become such a preemptive management goal. The competition with leading European and Asian companies for global, not just national, markets has required the large-scale overhauling of companies with much higher labor rates and overhead than their foreign counterparts. What's more, the exigencies of meeting financial analysts' expectations and shareholder demands for quarterly returns on their investments require efficiency above all. Ford's Annual Report of 1995 is typical in underscoring its commitment to greater "efficiency" 11 times in 11 pages, echoing Henry Ford's obsession with efficiency in constructing his assembly line nearly a century ago. Among other mentions, there is operational efficiency, cost efficiency, distribution efficiency, manufacturing efficiency, and investment efficiency.

We are hardly surprised, then, by the prevalence of free-market advocates, who hold that the sole responsibility of business today is to allocate resources in the most efficient manner. In a recent article, Herbert Stein, former chairman of the President's Council of Economic Advisers, argues that the only real "social responsibility" businesspeople have is "to run a corporation efficiently to maximize profits." According to Stein, efficiency "is not the only objective of life. . . . But it is the one that private corporations are best qualified to serve."[7]

If we accept the argument that efficiency is corporate America's top priority, if not its sole reason for being, then why can we not maintain that laws that inhibit efficiency in a free-market economy are really arbitrary? Holman Jenkins, a columnist for the *Wall Street Journal*, argues that the government's indictment of Archer Daniels Midland Company for price-fixing was based on a false assumption—namely, "that price-fixing harms the public." "No one is forced to buy lysine" [Archer Daniels' product], he argues, "and if lysine makers are gouging, new . . . and more efficient . . . competitors are free to enter the market."[8]

The implication that existing rules and regulations are sometimes irrelevant or inadequate attests the strength of our attachment to efficiency as the corporate lodestar of the 1990s. Taken as an end in itself, however, efficiency can obscure or threaten other equally important values. Maintaining the quality of life in the workplace, a sense of loyalty within the organization, and a concern for human dignity are among them.

The fictions of business, I contend, are indispensable in revealing the costs, in human terms, of an inordinate emphasis on efficiency. The examples I have chosen for discussion all happen to have been written before 1940. Dos Passos's *The Big Money,* Upton Sinclair's *The Jungle,* and Sinclair Lewis' *Babbitt* seem only to reflect an earlier era, far removed from our own high-tech, global-networking world. In rereading them after many years, though, I am struck by the trenchant commentary they offer on our own infatuation with efficiency. All of them compel us as custodians of efficient organizations to hold ourselves to account at a time when efficiency exerts such a powerful, if not tyrannical, grip on our collective thinking.

The Quintessential Efficiency Expert: Sinclair Lewis's *Babbitt*

No writer that I know of has mirrored American middle-class life in a commercially driven culture as unforgettably as Sinclair Lewis, who won the Nobel Prize for Literature in 1930. Lewis's *Babbitt,* published in 1922, is a satiric portrait of a provincial businessman in a medium-sized city called Zenith.[9] So widely read was Lewis's portrait of his novel's eponymous hero that for many years the name *Babbitt* was synonymous with all business and professional people who lead lives of stultifying conformity and smug self-satisfaction.

Lewis spent two years on trains, in hotel lobbies, and on street corners in midwestern cities recording his first-hand impressions of businesspeople, particularly how they were apt to think and behave in groups. Recurrent in their conversation was the term *efficiency*, which to Lewis's trained ear had so permeated the business culture of the time as to become synonymous with respectability and integrity.

As a social satirist, Lewis's technique is one of deliberate exaggeration, so that the salient characteristics of his small-town American characters stand out in bold relief. The man who invokes, but hardly embodies, efficiency as an ideal, George Babbitt, strikes the reader as both comic and pathetic. Babbitt is a realtor, who (like all the good realtors *I've* known) is "nimble in the calling of selling houses for more than people could afford to pay." Lewis's central character is scrupulous about conforming to what he *thinks* his fellow businessmen think he should say and do.

Even the most trivial personal accouterments contribute to Babbitt's sense of himself as the efficient "modern business man" and "Solid Citizen."

> Most significant of all was his loose-leaf pocket note-book, that modern and *efficient* note-book which contained the addresses of people whom he had forgotten, prudent memoranda of postal money-orders which had reached their destinations months ago, stamps which had lost their mucilage, . . . notes to be sure and do things which he did not intend to do. . . . (B, 9–10)

How deftly Sinclair Lewis suggests that, although Babbitt might prize efficiency in principle, he instinctively resists it in practice.

In Babbitt's lexicon, efficiency is integral to his glorification of Zenith as the "finest example of American life and prosperity to be found anywhere." His address to the annual meeting of the Zenith Real Estate Board on the virtues of efficiency is a compendium of clichés, catchphrases, and idiocies real enough to anyone who has ever had to sit through an after-dinner speech by someone who loves the sound of his or her own voice.

> . . . the modern American business man knows how to talk right up for himself. . . . He doesn't have to call in some highbrow hired-man when it's necessary for him to answer the crooked critics of the sane and *efficient* life. He's not dumb, like the old-fashioned merchant. He's got a vocabulary and a punch. (B, 183)

How can a man call himself a man, furthermore, let alone set the standard for good citizenship, without "earnest efficient endeavor"?

> It's here in Zenith, the home for manly men . . . that you find the largest proportion of these Regular Guys. . . . that's why Zenith will be remembered in history as having set the pace for a civilization that will endure when the old time-killing ways are gone forever and the day of earnest *efficient* endeavor shall have dawned all round the world! (B, 184)

Babbitt's equating of efficiency with sanity and manhood is mindless cant, laughable but also a little scary. For Babbitt and his self-righteous tribe would make pariahs of all those who fail to conform to their narrow mold. Foremost among the offenders is the liberal professor at the state university:

Those profs are the snakes to be scotched—they and all their milk-and-water ilk! The American business man is generous to a fault, but one thing he does demand of all teachers and lecturers and journalists: if we're going to pay them our good money, they've got to help us by selling *efficiency* and whooping it up for rational prosperity! (B, 187–188)

In lampooning the go-getter mentality, Lewis shows how a concept, mindlessly accepted, can so easily become not simply a harmless catchword, but an accepted cure-all for whatever ails a commercially driven society. To the casual reader, Babbitt may seem a cartoonish figure from a bygone era. I see him, though, as a frightening example of how we can embrace an idea without understanding the strength of its hold on us. As believers that efficiency is the capstone of our much heralded free-market system throughout the world, we need to remind ourselves of our capacity to denigrate competing values.

My concern here is that, in our zeal to make our businesses ever more efficient for the sake of ensuring what Darwin called a *competitive advantage*, we run the risk of losing our perspective on ourselves. In a revealing piece in *The New Yorker*, Adam Gopnik discussed how dismayed the French are at the self-congratulatory mood of American free-marketers and their trumpeting of corporate self-interest and efficiency:

After a recent trip to New York, one French journalist remarked that leafing through a copy of *Forbes* or *Fortune*

is like reading the operating manual of a strangely sanctimonious pirate ship.[10]

While we might disagree that "social security and social sol-
idarity weigh more than efficiency," as one French industrialist stated, disregarding alternative values can make us
unthinkingly narrow and self-righteous. Sinclair Lewis
would have insisted that we get the culture we deserve.

Sinclair Lewis, Meet Alfred P. Sloan

That Lewis's satire on the "selling" of "the sane and efficient"
life is pertinent both to his own time and to ours becomes
evident if we turn to a book about business management
that recalls the Babbitt era, and, at the same time, has an
ongoing appeal to a new generation likewise weaned on efficiency. Alfred P. Sloan's *My Years with General Motors* is one
of the classic texts on the development of corporate management. It was first published in 1963, years after Sloan had
retired as CEO of General Motors.[11] In articulating the
practical advantages of efficiency, which he introduced to
GM at its inception in the early twenties, Sloan and his
book have exerted a marked influence both on corporate
leaders and on business school curricula. His book was reissued in 1990, with fresh endorsements from Bill Gates and
Peter Drucker. (Drucker: "It is, I still maintain, the best
management book. . . ." [GM, x])

Trained as an electrical engineer, Sloan, like his great
rival Henry Ford, was understandably wed to efficiency, and

his book predictably reflects his single-minded pursuit of that industrial polestar: "The problem of development of the automobile was to raise its level of efficiency. . . ." (GM, 220). Both automobile titans were the beneficiaries of Frederick Taylor's earlier researches into what Taylor was to term *scientific management*. Taylor has been hailed as the "Apostle of the American Gospel of Efficiency" for his pioneering work in breaking down factory operations into their simplest tasks and then timing workers to determine the speediest and most cost-effective way to perform a given operation.

Sloan, like Ford, embraced this new, "scientific" way of organizing work with enthusiasm, but the loss of individual initiative and demoralization of the workforce are not evident in his paean to efficiency. The historian Daniel Boorstin, in his discussion of mass-production techniques at General Motors, reminds us of these downsides:

> By mid-century, General Motors, in its contracts with its workers, had divided the hour into six-minute periods, had fragmented the work to fit the periods, and the worker was being paid by the number of tenths of an hour that he worked. . . . If the worker was paid by the tenth of an hour for performing his task precisely as prescribed, then he would have no need and little opportunity for initiative. And the fractioning of work by the new calculus of scientific management would make the meaning and the value of the factory-worker's exertions harder than ever for the worker himself to understand.[12]

If there is an awareness of such problems, we do not find any acknowledgment of it in *My Years with General Motors*. Quite the contrary: Sloan's aim is to extend the concept of efficiency to all levels of "professional management." Developing "a common measure of efficiency with which to judge the contribution of each [GM] division to the whole," and exerting pressure "to maintain the efficiency required to maintain cost objectives" are now staples of Management 101.

That efficiency is the linchpin of success, not just at General Motors but also in American industry generally is Sloan's overriding theme:

> Most successful enterprises in American industry have tended to grow. General Motors obviously is a successful enterprise. It is successful because it is efficient, and it has grown accordingly. (GM, 436)

This kind of categorical statement is omnipresent in Sloan's discussion of efficiency. If, in his words, the "strategic aim of a business is to earn a return on capital investment," then it is only by discovering exactly where the "efficiencies and inefficiencies" in the overall organization lie that you have "an objective basis for the allocation of new investment."

In his concluding chapter, Sloan states that efficiency is the "end product of what I have described in this book." In saying this, he has another motive, which is to preserve the advantages of a free-market economy against the depredations that government regulation—in the form of antitrust measures, for example—might conceivably wreak on big business:

> I hold that General Motors' efficiency and growth are interrelated in our highly competitive economy. And I

hold that if companies are attacked simply because they are big then an attack on efficiency must be a corollary of that attack. If we penalize efficiency, how can we as a nation compete in the economy of the world? (GM, 443)

This is precisely the argument that holds sway in the late 1990s, where the need to be competitive "in the economy of the world" has made corporate mass, coupled with a laissez-faire policy, seem mandatory. Certainly the current rash of megamergers and acquisitions, tacitly if not directly sanctioned by the government, would seem to make Sloan's position that efficiency ranks highest among corporate values the prevailing one.

All well and not so good. I remain persnickety on Sloan's view of corporate priorities because values that are less hard-edged than efficiency tend to get lost in our collective mind, as Sinclair Lewis, for one, well knew. As proof, we need only look at the attitudes toward business values on the part of Sloan's heirs, the next generation of managers and executives who have been raised primarily on the gospel of efficiency over the past decade or so.

What Is the Primary Responsibility of a Company?

A 1996 study by the Johnson Graduate School of Management at Cornell University contrasted attitudes on corporate priorities between MBA students and senior executives from Fortune 1000 companies. While both agreed that the financial strength of a company is a paramount consideration, 86 percent of the students felt that maximizing profits is a company's primary responsibility, while only 75 percent of the executives felt that way, and one out of four opposed the idea. The difference may not seem significant, except that corporate leaders have already taken a harder line on maximizing profits through operating efficiencies than they did some years ago. The dean of the Johnson School commented, "Executives are increasingly concerned with soft skills, such as how to nurture and develop employees, get the most out of teams, deal with the social issues that arise from being located in communities, and develop leadership. Students, on the other hand, don't appear to appreciate fully the importance of those issues."[13] Most revealing, and consistent with this attitude, was the students' feeling that compassion would be a very minor component of corporate leadership in 2006. On this issue there was a significant 20-point spread.

If I were charged with trying to leaven the austere values of the current generation of MBAs, I think I would require them to read John Dos Passos's unique portrait of Henry Ford in his novel *The Big Money*, published in 1937.[14] The work as a whole is an indictment of the American capitalistic system, which the writer saw as blighting the lives of so many Americans during the Depression era. For Dos Passos, only the predatory and the self-seeking could hope to prevail under a dehumanizing system. Agree or not, you must nevertheless reckon with Dos Passos's compelling recreation of Henry Ford's pursuit of efficiency at all—mostly human—costs.

The account of Ford appears in the form of a minibiography, one of several set-pieces interspersed among the fic-

tional episodes in *The Big Money* for the purpose of high-
lighting a recurrent theme in the work as a whole. "Tin
Lizzie" is the title of the Ford biography and refers to the
popular name for the famous Model T. The piece is written
in a semidocumentary style with details artfully selected to
dramatize the dire human consequences of Ford's adoption
of mass-production methods. Chief among these is the mov-
ing assembly line that seemed to vindicate the new passion
for efficiency. No merely factual or journalistic account can
match Dos Passos's recreation, in his characteristically dead-
pan and ironic voice, of the momentum of the efficiency
movement (the "Taylor Plan") and the natural resistance to
it on the part of Ford's employees:

> In these years the Taylor Plan was stirring up plantman-
> agers and manufacturers all over the country. Efficiency
> was the word. The same ingenuity that went into improv-
> ing the performance of a machine could go into improving
> the performance of the workmen producing the machine.
>   In 1913 they established the assembly line at Ford's.
> That season the profits were something like twentyfive
> million dollars, but they had trouble in keeping the men
> on the job, machinists didn't seem to like it at Ford's.
> (TBM, 50)

To improve morale, thereby increasing productivity,
and, indirectly, to stimulate demand for the Model T on the
part of the factory worker who could otherwise ill afford it,
Ford took the unprecedented step of raising the daily pay for
his workers to five dollars. This was, to all appearances, an
act of munificence. The man who prided himself on the

"democratization" of the motor car, however, tried to impose his puritanical system of values on his employees with the zeal of an autocrat. As Dos Passos was quick to see, this compounded the regimentation dictated by efficiency:

> The American Plan; automotive prosperity seeping down
> from above; it turned out there were strings to it.
>   But that five dollars a day
>   paid to good, clean American workmen
>   who didn't drink or smoke cigarettes or read or
> think,
>   and who didn't commit adultery
>   and whose wives didn't take in boarders,
>   made America once more the Yukon of the
> sweated workers of the world;
>   made all the tin lizzies and the automotive age,
> and incidentally,
>   made Henry Ford the automobileer, the admirer
> of Edison, the birdlover,
>   the great American of his time. (TBM, 51)

In the rhythms of his prose, Dos Passos captures the soul-deadening monotony of labor requisite to an efficient operation and to the greater glory of Henry Ford and American enterprise:

> . . . in 1922 Henry Ford sold one million three hundred
> and thirtytwo thousand two hundred and nine tin lizzies;
> he was the richest man in the world.
>   Good roads had followed the narrow ruts made in the
> mud by the Model T. The great automotive boom was on.

At Ford's production was improving all the time; less waste, more spotters, strawbosses, stool-pigeons (fifteen minutes for lunch, three minutes to go to the toilet, the Taylorized speedup everywhere, reach under, adjust washer, screw down bolt, shove in cotterpin, reachunder adjustwasher, screwdown bolt, reachunderadjustscrewdownreachunderadjust until every ounce of life was sucked off into production and at night the workmen went home grey shaking husks). (*TBM*, 55)

Dos Passos's real target was not efficiency as such, but the messianic fervor with which Ford pursued it. It would actually be more accurate to say that, for the writer, Ford was less a messiah than an Antichrist. For what was unconscionable to Dos Passos's way of thinking was an industrial system that degraded its human components even as it made for productivity and profitability on an unheard-of scale.

I wonder if, after reading Dos Passos, the future captains of industry would continue to give such a lowly ranking to compassion and such a high priority to maximizing profits via efficiency in their assessment of corporate priorities in the twenty-first century. True, Alfred Sloan may well have owed much of his success to his being so clear and definite about what the chief responsibility of General Motors should be:

The primary object of the corporation . . . we declared was to make money, not just to make motor cars. (*GM*, 64)

Today's top echelon at Ford is similarly single-minded: Its announced "primary purpose" is "serving the interests of our shareholders by providing them with an excellent return for their money." Who would take issue with these positions in view of America's overall economic hegemony?

Without downplaying the paramount importance of being profitable and creating shareholder value, I would emphasize that there are effective ways to achieve these ends other than through efficiency per se. In fact, I would argue that if I had to rank, in order of strategic importance, serving the interests of your shareholders, your customers, and your employees, I would reverse the order in which I have listed them here. Creating and sustaining a loyal and committed workforce can go a long way, I believe, toward generating greater customer satisfaction and, by extension, greater shareholder wealth.

I am by no means alone in this view. Hewlett-Packard is a conspicuous example of how corporate priorities that have little to do with profitability and efficiency as such have made the company one of the most successful in America, by any standards.

John Young, Hewlett-Packard CEO from 1976 to 1992, said in an interview on his company's priorities:

> Maximizing shareholder wealth has always been way down the list. Yes, profit is a cornerstone of what we do—it is a measure of our contribution and a means of self-financed growth—but it has never been the *point* in and of itself. The point, in fact, is to *win*, and winning is judged in the eyes of the customer and by doing something you can be proud of. There is a symmetry of logic in this. If we provide real satisfaction to real customers—we will be profitable. . . .[15]

In discussing why the company he founded exists in the first place, David Packard said the following:

> I think many people assume, wrongly, that a company exists simply to make money. While this is an important result of a company's existence, we have to go deeper and find the real reasons for our being. . . . we inevitably come to the conclusion that a group of people get together and exist as an institution that we call a company so they are able to accomplish something collectively that they could not accomplish separately—they make a contribution to society, a phrase which sounds trite but is fundamental. . . .[16]

As pragmatic executives, we might object that Packard's philosophical rationales, however noble, are no substitute for efficiency in coping with day-to-day exigencies. As a matter of corporate responsibility, though, we must still ask how, exactly, managers can temper their passion for operational efficiency with a sense of shared purpose and a concern for the individuals on whom a healthy rate of productivity depends.

Achieving Efficiency Through Consensus

In the middle of the Great Depression, when Dos Passos was writing about the pitfalls of the efficiency movement, Maidenform's brassiere business, then a decade old, was booming. Since the bra was an affordable, low-ticket item priced for a mass market and had become a staple in women's wardrobes, it was relatively Depression-proof. Maidenform found itself in an enviable position for a manufacturing company at the time because the demand for its product far exceeded the available supply. A much more efficient sewing operation was therefore required to fill the retailers' orders.

The challenge for the company was to raise the output of the 400-odd sewing machine operators that Maidenform then employed at its plant in Bayonne, New Jersey. The executives in charge of production had struggled without success to find a way to create incentives for the operators under the hourly wage system, then common in the garment industry. At the time, most of the workers were performing at only 50 to 60 percent of their possible efficiency. No surprise there. People were paid the same wage regardless of how quickly they worked. If the company could get them up to 100 percent, though, it would benefit from greater overall output and become more efficient in its utilization of equipment and overhead.

Instead of further tinkering with the hourly-wage system, Maidenform decided to adopt a system that at the time was unprecedented in women's apparel. Time and motion studies that Taylor had introduced would be used to establish a piecework system geared to benefit both the company and its operators. Now piecework, according to which operators are paid by the number of units they produce rather than by the hour, was not uncommon in the industry. The standards set, however, were invariably the result of a negotiation with the International Ladies Garment Workers Union (ILGWU) instead of the time and motion studies that Frederick Taylor had introduced to American industry.

Overzealous efficiency experts in the textile and auto-
motive industries, among others, had already created bad
feelings about the new, efficient methods of "scientific management." Sherwood Anderson, a well-known writer of the
time, was as sensitive as Dos Passos to the humiliations
suffered by workers under the tyranny of the stopwatch. Fol-
lowing a visit to a Southern cotton mill, he wrote a dev-
astating account of a "minute-man" hovering for hours over
a weaver's every move and even timing her visits to the
restroom. At the time, Maidenform purchased its raw mate-
rials from the very mills which so aroused Anderson's indignation.

The problem for the company lay less in the technical
problem of applying the time/study methods themselves
than in convincing suspicious union officials that Maidenform's implementation of the new scientific techniques
would be humane and fair to the workers. Equally important
to union resistance was the fear of losing its power to nego-
tiate in the matter of rate-setting and thereby forfeiting a
degree of control. The key, therefore, was to understand the
union's motivation for resistance.

The ILGWU sent over one of its own industrial engineers to appraise the company's analysis and recommendations. The company's executives spent several days with
him, at the end of which time he concluded, predictably,
that the system had some merits but that negotiation was
the way to set standards. The company then wrote an
answering brief to his objections, the result of which was
that an independent arbitrator was chosen jointly by Maidenform and the ILGWU to decide the matter. Again, the
company spent about a week going over the methods and

criteria for the proposed time studies, anticipating some of the objections to the program they knew would arise. The result was that the arbitrator found Maidenform's plans to be favorable to the operators.

Contrary to prevailing industry practice, for example, the company promised that, once a rate for an operator was set, that rate would not be changed. Besides being fair to the individual operators, this policy made good practical sense. After all, if a worker overproduced and then found that the rate had been cut, any incentive she might have to beat the standard would be eliminated. To change the rate would thus be self-defeating. Although the company might pay too much for a particular operation, it would still gain in the utilization of equipment and overhead, especially in comparison with the former hourly system.

Even when supply caught up with demand, Maidenform never wavered in its principle of adherence to the rates it had set. What the company gained thereby was the valuable trust and loyalty of its operators. In a Darwinian world, "trust" and "loyalty" may sound quaintly old-fashioned. But in securing these intangible assets early, Maidenform forged a long-term bond with its employees, the practical advantages of which included comparatively low turnover rates in its manufacturing facilities, low overall training costs, and low downtime. Not bad things at all if the goal is a truly efficient operation.

Consistent with the company's sincere regard for its employees during this period was that its executives carefully avoided an autocratic imposition of a new, untried system. Training sessions were held on the sewing floor with the foremen and the union representatives present. The purpose of these sessions was to allow everyone involved to observe the time/study principles in action prior to implementation, so that they could see what allowances were being made for downtime, leisure-time and the like. Furthermore, time/study methods would be introduced gradually, one floor at a time.

Maidenform also profited from the techniques of scientific management in ways that it could *not* have anticipated at the time. The company thought it chose wisely in initiating the time/study program on a sewing floor where there was a popular and highly regarded manager. What it discovered after the new system was up and running was that this outgoing and charming individual was really a "seat-of-the-pants" manager, with little ability to conform to the newer, more accurate methods for measuring and monitoring an operator's output. What the company learned from this experiment still holds: An engaging personality can often cause us to overlook basic deficiencies in a manager.

In one sense, though, the nontechnical aspects of the radical new program were less critical to its successful implementation than cultural variances. Taylor's principles of "scientific management" provided little guidance to the company's engineers in anticipating the reactions of the young female sewing machine operators in the New Jersey plant. Incentive pay earned by the more competent operators might mean little to them if they were obliged, as the company knew they were, to turn over their paychecks to their husbands or families to help them meet household expenses. The company therefore devised the method of putting their basic salary in one envelope and their bonus money in another. That way, they got to keep whatever they earned over and above their base pay. Though not foolproof, this simple system helped initially in launching the piece-work process.

In short, the company made every effort, not just to impose a more efficient system on its operators, but, step-by-step, to demonstrate to them that *they*, too, would benefit from its initiatives. The company's idea of "customer service" (before the term became a managerial cliché) was, in effect, to regard the workers as its most valued customers. The principle was simple: A motivated and loyal workforce will be inherently efficient, thus providing better service to its retail customers.

This account of Maidenform's formative period comes from Abe Kanner, an executive with the company for 62 years, and one of the people responsible for the adroit and humane manner in which the efficiency program was handled. Abe is a living example of how to apply the fictions of business to problems of management. Already steeped in the imaginative literature of the period when he joined the company in 1934, Abe told me that these writers sensitized him to the human problems that arose from manufacturers' passion for efficiency, and he characterized himself as an idealist at the time. Prompted by his reading, he combined his idealism with his practical know-how to systematize an operation that owed its efficiency to a broad consensus on manufacturing ends and means.

One of the authors that had a marked influence on Abe was Upton Sinclair, whose novel, *The Jungle*, published in 1906, documented in grisly detail the plight of workers in the meat-packing industry in Chicago at the turn of the century.[17] I find Sinclair's work to have continuing relevance to the tyranny of efficiency in the 1990s.

Workplace "Jungles" Past and Present

The plot of The Jungle turns on the increasingly desperate efforts of a Lithuanian peasant family to find a means of subsistence in a country that everywhere exploits them. Naive and illiterate, they are easy prey to exploitation by real estate agents, local merchants, and most of all, their employers in the meat-packing industry. Held to pitiful wages, a mind-numbing routine, and physically exhausting and hazardous jobs, the Rudkus family experiences a slow, inevitable decline at the hands of a system that is rife with corruption and self-aggrandizement and that regards human beings as disposable. The novel's hero, Jurgis Rudkus, begins as an honest, hard-working, self-sacrificing *naif*, whose increasingly desperate life leads him to drink, petty crime, and collusion with the corrupt local politicians. His redemption comes when, by happenstance, he is initiated into a circle of Socialists, who give Jurgis a reason for being and the hope of taking control of his life.

Despite its deterministic scenario and its quixotic denouement (or perhaps because of them) The Jungle became an international best-seller. Sinclair's novel achieved the rarer feat, moreover, of prompting political action: more stringent government standards for food processing. His descriptions of how tubercular animals, spoiled meat, and

animal parts unfit for human consumption are processed
and sold as "Number One Grade" meat were based on personal observation. At the start of the novel, a guide who
shows the newly arrived Rudkus family through the meat-
packing plant remarks, "They use everything about the hog
except the squeal."

Efficiency, as Sinclair points out, is the crux of a system
that depends not simply on finding uses for all parts of the
animal "except the squeal," but on eliminating waste in
human labor as well. Before their initiation into the rigors
of work in the plant, the Rudkus family, awestruck by the
size and complexity of the operation, "thought only of the
wonderful efficiency of it all." The terrible irony, of course,
is that it is precisely the efficiency of the system that, far
from being their deliverance, as they at first suppose, will
enslave them and reduce them to an insensate, animal-like
state.

The heart of this dehumanizing process is the dreaded
"speeding up" on the line, a work-rate determined by that of
the strongest and fastest workers.

> The pace they set here, it was one that called for every
> faculty of a man—from the instant the first steer fell till
> the sounding of the noon whistle, and again from half
> past twelve till heaven only knew what hour in the late
> afternoon or evening, there was never one instant's rest
> for a man, for his hand or his eye or his brain. . . . they
> worked like men possessed. . . . and if any man could not
> keep up with the pace, there were hundreds outside beg-
> ging to try. (J, 71)

Nor is this inhuman pace a peculiarity of a single plant:

> "And every week the managers of it [the Beef Trust] got together and compared notes, and there was one scale for all the workers in the yards and one standard of efficiency." (J, 133)

This system has the further effect of directing a man's hostility not just at his boss but at his fellow workers:

> Underneath [the boss], ranged in ranks and grades like an army, were managers and superintendents and foremen, each one driving the man next below him and trying to squeeze out of him as much work as possible. And all the men of the same rank were pitted against each other; the accounts of each were kept separately, and every man lived in terror of losing his job, if another made a better record than he. So from top to bottom the place was simply a seething cauldron of jealousies and hatreds; there was no loyalty or decency anywhere about it, there was no place in it where a man counted for anything against a dollar. (J, 147)

In 1994, about 90 years after Sinclair wrote his harrowing exposé, the *Wall Street Journal* printed a report on conditions in the poultry industry in the South and briefly noted similarities to *The Jungle*. Some of those similarities, if we look at them more closely, are enough to make Sinclair's documentation of the costs of efficiency seem like a record of our time as well as his.

A standing joke among the poultry plant workers alludes to the efficiency in finding end-uses for all the parts—feathers, blood, viscera, and so forth: "They don't waste anything in a chicken plant—except the cackle." For Sinclair's illiterate immigrants, desperate for jobs, we may substitute today's unskilled workers in the rural South. And for the Beef Trust, the Chicken Trust, if we can call it that, notorious for paying subsistence wages and for a draconian "speeding up" of the line over the past 15 years.

Under these conditions, the dehumanization of a workforce that is helpless and ignorant of its rights is no less severe at the end of the twentieth century than at the beginning. The *Journal* report would seem to replicate *The Jungle* in documenting the agony of long hours on the line without a break, with workers penalized for unauthorized trips to the restroom. The reporter's description of how the assembly-line system pits one worker against another exposes a disregard for human dignity abetted by an unbridled passion for efficiency.

> "As in many factories, the conveyor belt sets the pace and anyone who flags creates more work for those farther down the line. So workers tend to vent their fatigue and frustration on each other."[18]

Both *The Jungle* and the *Journal* article suggest that the lack of concern for the human costs of efficiency is not peculiar to the plant management, but is also tacitly condoned by government regulators. In *The Jungle*, any attempt at promoting reform on the part of government inspectors is frustrated by the plant managers, who bribe or intimidate them, or disguise the wretched working conditions. According to the *Journal*, neither today's government nor the poultry plant management considered "worker safety when ramping up speeds; rather, processors seem to have convinced regulators that they could move chickens faster without sacrificing food hygiene." Were Upton Sinclair alive today to comment on the *Journal* exposé, he would surely be as indignant as he was in his own time to see so much attention being paid to pure food standards and so little to the plight of the poultry processors.

The Ultimate Time-Study Techie: Mark Twain's *A Connecticut Yankee in King Arthur's Court*

Perhaps the best corrective to an overzealous pursuit of self-interest and efficiency in a "survival-of-the-fittest" culture is a healthy sense of the absurd. In *A Connecticut Yankee in King Arthur's Court* (1889), Mark Twain exposes the pretensions and great foolishness of an efficiency expert who uses Yankee know-how to exploit the unknowing and make a quick buck.

Twain's back-to-the-future novel is about a late-nineteenth-century time-study technician named Hank Morgan. . . . who inexplicably wakes to find himself in sixth-century Camelot after being accidentally hit over the head by a wrench.[19] Morgan is quick to see the advantage he has over a people who, from his point of view, are ignorant and superstitious. In his efforts to win over the populace, he quickly gets the better of his chief adversary, Merlin, by predicting and then "producing" an eclipse of the sun that his hindsight tells him must occur on a given date. The people are in awe of his magic, and Morgan, leveraging his power, sets himself up as "Sir Boss."

Twain's central character, a true Darwinian, also has an entrepreneurial bent, and he quickly figures out how to gain a competitive advantage by adapting himself supremely well to his new environment. One day he comes upon a group of hermits doing perpetual penance through abstinence and, in some cases, self-flagellation. One of these individuals is "a mighty celebrity" who has been praying nonstop for 20 years atop a 60-foot pillar, "bowing his body ceaselessly and rapidly almost to his feet." Morgan at once sees his opportunity to exploit the hermit for commercial purposes:

> I timed him with a stopwatch, and he made twelve hundred and forty-four revolutions in twenty-four minutes and forty-six seconds. It seemed a pity to have all this power going to waste. It was one of the most useful motions in mechanics, the pedal movement; so I made a note in my memorandum book, purposing some day to apply a system of elastic cords to him and run a sewing machine with it. I afterwards carried out that scheme and got five years' good service out of him; in which time he turned out upwards of eighteen thousand first-rate tow-linen shirts, which was ten a day. (CY, 148)

Morgan works his saint on Sundays, too ("it was no use to waste the power"). He finds that by creatively marketing the shirts "as a perfect protection against sin," he makes money hand over fist. Even saints have their limits, of

184 FICTIONS OF BUSINESS

course, and Morgan's saint expires within a year, though not before Morgan has introduced a line extension ("goods suitable for kings"). Morgan willingly gives the saint his due:

> . . . the good saint got him to his rest. But he had earned
> it. I can say that for him. (CY, 149)

The fictions of business never let us forget that there are limitations to the pursuit of self-interest and efficiency, however vital these may be to surviving in an acquisitive and highly competitive culture. To the extent that we fail to balance self-interest with a sense of responsibility to the people we employ and manage, and to balance our passion for efficiency with a sensitivity to fundamental human needs and civilities, we increasingly demean ourselves. At all times, the key to keeping fit in a Darwinian world is constantly to remind ourselves of the qualities and values that distinguish us from the lower animals, that make us most fully human.

✒ 6 ✑

OFFICE POLITICS, STRESS MANAGEMENT, AND CHAOS

"The inclination to aggression . . . constitutes the greatest impediment to civilization. . . . Necessity alone, the advantages of work in common, will not hold men together."
Sigmund Freud, *Civilization and Its Discontents*

It was just about a week to the day since Mr. Martin had decided to rub out Mrs. Ulgine Barrows—
James Thurber, "The Catbird Seat"

T oday the level of stress induced by restructuring and downsizing exacerbates interpersonal conflicts and makes them harder to handle. Job insecurity and the devaluation of traditional loyalty between employees and their companies can only stimulate resentments. We increasingly hear horror stories—I mean that literally— about the lengths people will go to to vent their frustration and anger. One that drew my attention recently was a *Wall Street Journal* account of how Dale Windsor, former president of Coffman Industries, fired a 56-year-old woman who was the company's head of finance for "alleged embezzlement."

> Hours later, the woman showed up at his office and shot him through the groin with a .38-caliber pistol. She continued to fire at Mr. Windsor, 47, as the martial arts–trained executive leaped over furniture to evade the bullets. She is currently serving a three-year prison term for charges stemming from the assault.[1]

There are a few things about this account that cry out for explanation. How could Mr. Windsor, trained for action though he was, have kept hurtling over the office furniture *after* being shot in the groin? Equally puzzling, while the president's physical agility commands respect, his reported reflection on the incident, at least on the face of it, seems obtuse for an experienced executive, especially in today's hypersensitive climate:

> When you're terminating a man, you're always on your guard that they could get excited. But with a woman who's 56 years old, you don't expect anything to happen.

To be on the safe side, perhaps it's best to assume, per Murphy's Law, that if anything *can* happen in a corporate office, it will. Managing irrational disputes, whatever their severity, is an art that requires all the human understanding you can muster. We need only look at our own native biases and assorted blind-spots to gauge fully how hard it is to see and evaluate others objectively. I have found the fictions of business to be unerring, if unorthodox, guides to the often hidden motives underlying the wayward behavior that prevents managers from working together effectively.

Managing Conflict Irresolution: Wilfred Sheed's *Office Politics*

Sheed's book, published in 1966, was a runner-up that year for the National Book Award.[2] It is a comic novel about interpersonal conflicts in a publishing house that puts out a weekly liberal journal, *The Outsider*, with a limited circulation. The central characters are the editor, an Englishman called Gilbert Twining, two long-time associate editors named Brian Fine and Fritz Tyler, and a recently hired junior editor named George Wren, who quickly becomes the confidant of all the others.

The novelist is quick to emphasize the contrast between *The Outsider's* liberal bent and the illiberal personal sentiments that motivate its editorial staff. What Twining, the chief editor, calls "the most *civilized* magazine in the United States" ill accords with the editors' uncivil impulses toward each other. Twining and his two senior editors, Fine and Tyler, spar incessantly over what gets to be included in the weekly number, and who gets to approve the final copy. Underlying this ongoing debate, though, are personal issues of *control* and *power*.

Sensitivities run high in this office, to the point of paranoia. In quick succession, each of the three senior editors privately vents his feelings about the others to the politically neutral junior editor, George Wren. First, the editor-in-chief, Twining, on his conniving number two and three editors, Tyler and Fine:

> "They hate my insides, you see". . . . They imagine that they are solely responsible for a magazine's success. They begin to have editorial ideas. They send you memos. You ignore them and poof!"—George couldn't conjure up the rest right now; it gave him a headache. (OP, 7)

Next, Tyler, an adept at insinuation, on his boss, Twining:

> "And what do you think of the maestro?" asked Fritz.
> "Mr. Twining?". . . . I think he's a fine editor. Don't you?"
> "Oh yeah, no doubt about it. And such a distinguished man. Maybe he's not as good as he was. Which of us is? You go stale in this business. . . . We've had a couple of dull issues, and it always begins to look like the end. Gilbert is basically a pro, so I guess he'll pull us out. If not—poof, as we French say." (OP, 9)

George Wren's growing feeling at this point that he is part of a "charade" is then confirmed when the number three editor, Brian Fine, also takes him into his confidence:

> "And the captain [Twining], what do you make of him?"
> "A quite marvelous man. Peerless type." . . .

> "Of course, Twining is certainly a first-class man. No doubt at all. But I sometimes feel that he takes on too much, if you know what I mean."

"I don't know what you mean. Too much what?"

"You must have noticed that *The Outsider* is basically a one-man show. We haven't had an editorial meeting in two months. The whole magazine expresses one man's personality. And however interesting that man may be—" (*OP*, 12–13)

Amidst this innuendo, one thing is clear: The CEO has the edge, provided he is pragmatic and calculating, as Sheed's Gilbert Twining proves to be:

His only hold on them was personal ascendancy; and that was something that he had to hoard like a miser. . . . But how much personal ascendancy did one have? Carefully rationed, how long would it last? (*OP*, 17–18)

The operative word here is the reiterated "personal." For the real issues among the editors are personal rather than professional. The deteriorating relationship between Twining and Brian Fine shows us how readily smoldering resentments undermine working relationships. Seven years before, Twining, then the newly appointed chief editor, had offered Fine what he felt was some constructive criticism. From Twining's point of view, he had gone on to transform Fine "from a sentimental windbag . . . into a reasonably competent editor." Twining now reflects ruefully on the incident:

[He] had been incredibly excruciatingly gentle with Fine—you could hardly make any points at all with less force—and Fine had gone stiff all over, very nearly burst into tears as well; and had nursed the grievance for seven long years since. (*OP*, 66)

This is a classic no-win situation. If we take Twining's reflection at face value, nothing could have prevented Fine's hypersensitive reaction to criticism. Fine, for his part, has always resented Twining's criticisms as patronizing:

> "These [Fine's editorials] won't do, you know," said Twining. The awful little phrase. For the next two hours, Twining had gone through the damn editorials with him like examination papers, paragraph by paragraph, and every moment was painful. But Brian couldn't get past that first phrase. "These won't do, you know, Won't do, you know." . . . Twining had remained impeccably friendly and polite throughout. Having ripped every bit of skin off his associate editor, having shredded his personality into blinders, he was more than willing to act as if nothing had happened. (*OP*, 62)

We need only reflect on how the smallest grievances, springing—yes, even from a phrase or tone of voice—can fester. And how our failure to have an honest conversation when called for can transform professional differences of opinion into personal affronts. And how every subsequent encounter then becomes cause for offense. At one point, Fine, having discovered that Twining had shortened one of his pieces, equates Twining's action with emasculation:

> Brian Fine looked at his truncated editorial, holy men's room, what had Twining wrought this time? Brian had worked for three days whittling three paragraphs on the race question, building carefully to a crescendo of outrage—and here Twining had gone and snipped off the

crescendo: siphoned off the outrage. This couldn't be good editing, could it? . . .

Brian took his castrated editorial back to his cubicle. (*OP*, 33–34)

As an astute observer of human foibles, Wilfred Sheed knows that people will always take the moral high road, if they can. Self-justification is universal. In Fine's case, it has a rebounding effect. Entering into his character's head, Sheed exposes a familiar managerial ploy: the effort to conceal personal animosity by telling yourself that you are acting, as the saying goes, "in the best interests of the business." Fine reflects:

> He [Fine] wasn't some sort of Iago-like plotter, just a man trying to help out a magazine. People were doing it all over town—in all those great morose buildings on both sides of the street, it was plot, plot, plot—cutting out tiny cancers like Twining, to keep the larger organisms alive. It was honestly nothing personal. (*OP*, 32)

Of *course* not.

Fritz Tyler, the number two editor, shows similar ingenuity in justifying himself at the expense of his boss, Twining. In the midst of wooing the magazine's chief financial backer to further his career, Tyler reflects that his motives "for making out with Mrs. Wadsworth . . . weren't all high-minded ones." It is the warmth he shows her as a "human being," however, that purportedly makes him a worthier editor than Twining:

> It was precisely this difference between himself and Twin-
> ing that convinced him that Twining's liberalism was
> nothing but attitude; which in turn accounted for *The
> Outsider's* tinny ring these days. (*OP*, 39)

Real mastery of office politics, Sheed goes on to demonstrate, involves more than an ability on Twining's part to
handle day-to-day skirmishes with his editors. Real mastery
is knowing how to overcome threats to your authority when
prompted by untoward circumstances. Midway through his
story, the author raises the stakes in the game of office politics. The chief editor, Twining, has a heart attack while on a
business trip. Thinking that Twining is out of the picture for
good, Fine and Tyler vie for the top job.

Without consulting anyone, Fine arrogates full editorial
authority to himself and fills a key position with an inept
nephew. Tyler, meanwhile, continues to pay court to the
chief financial backer of the magazine, promising to print
her inane theater reviews on the pages of *The Outsider* in
hopes that she will back him as chief editor.

Before anyone gets very far in his maneuvering, Sheed
has Twining reappear on the scene. With George Wren in
tow, Twining pays a series of weekend calls to his staff, beginning with a late-night visit to a nervously expectant Brian
Fine. Under the veneer of gentility and the pretense of having time to kill, the chief editor strings Fine out by talking
chit-chat and then by complimenting him on the job Fine
did in his absence. But there is no mistaking his tone:

> "Well now, the magazine." Twining sounded humorously
> businesslike, like a chairman on an amateur committee.

"It looks to me as if you've all done quite a creditable job in my absence . . . Simply keeping the flag flying is no small triumph. . . . Let me congratulate you on your presence of mind." . . .

Brian nodded under the lash of the compliment. (*OP*, 193)

With that, Twining mentions casually that he did "notice a few things," and opens the issue Fine edited that was "disfigured with red marks, as if Twining had been bleeding it back to health." Until 3 A.M., Twining bombards Fine with picayune criticisms of his work, peppered with "school-teacher asperities, patronizing and sarcastic." The technique is deadly:

George suddenly realized that Twining was cold-bloodedly wearing the man out. Since the specific criticisms were quite meaningless, it followed that the whole affair was an exercise in raw power. Twining could have made his marks at random on any issue; they were only a pretext for beating up Brian.

Brian looked up in puffy despair. (*OP*, 195)

Sheed further shows Twining's adroitness in strengthening his power base by having his chief editor reinstate Wally Funk, Twining's regular drama critic for *The Outsider*, whom the scheming Tyler had fired in his absence. Funk is a sensitive peacock whose ego has been badly bruised, as Twining well knows. Twining's problem in getting him back to work for *The Outsider* is that, while Funk is an astute critic, his writing is florid and needs Twining's firm editorial hand to temper it. Twining makes this clear to Funk even as he disarms this vain man with the extravagant praise that Twining knows he craves:

> "You're a Dionysian writer, Wally, as I've told you so often. We disciples of Apollo must trim the exuberances at times. . . . But give me a Dionysian writer any day, with the blazing insights, the broad, flashing strokes. We drudges can do the pruning, the tidying up after the hurricane. . . ." Wally wriggled shamelessly in his chair; he was so pleased he didn't know where to hide it. (*OP*, 201)

How shamelessly, yet artfully, the wily editor pushes the emotional buttons of his wayward staff! Flattery can be a potent managerial weapon in motivating employees. It should be used, as Sheed suggests, not simply to make an employee feel good, but to keep him under friendly control. Funk, the drama critic, needs the praise at this point, but his deeper need, as both he and Twining know, is to return to the corporate womb. For George Wren, who is getting an education in guile, Twining's "cadences [in addressing Wally Funk] were almost those of mother and son," and "it was understood that Mother's word was final." Any executive who understands the value many people continue to place on the security corporate life provides will appreciate Twining's rhetorical strategy here.

Adjusting his approach to the particular individual is Twining's stock-in-trade as an executive. The chief editor further demonstrates his managerial virtuosity in bringing back his long-time advertising director, Philo Sonnabend, whom Brian Fine had abruptly replaced with his nephew.

Knowing that Sonnabend is a man who nurses resentments, he simply allows him to vent his spleen against the usurper Fine ("of course he didn't ask my advice about the ads, *oh no, not Brian*. . . ."). After Sonnabend has talked himself out, Twining regains the confidence of him and his wife by being suitably approving and contrite:

> Twining was silent a moment, and the Sonnabends watched him like musicians watching the conductor. . . .
>   "You were quite right to tell me," Twining said at last. "These things are unfortunate." He shook his head. "It's my fault for leaving things in such a confusion."
>   Philo relaxed and basked. (*QP*, 205–206)

We often hear that the ability to listen well is the mark of a good manager. Like all generalizations, that is true of certain situations but not of others. As a *superior* manager, Gilbert Twining knows when to talk and when to listen. Sheed's musical metaphor is apt; as a consummate "conductor," Twining knows that orchestrating his responses as the occasion warrants is the correct strategy.

The trickiest role-play of all for Twining is one that will put his scheming number two editor, Fritz Tyler, in his place. By offering the financial backer of the magazine a regular drama column (of course, she knows nothing about drama), Tyler has apparently won her support for his bid to become the new chief editor. Accompanied by George Wren, Twining visits Tyler and the woman in her apartment one Saturday night. Playing to the woman's vanity, Twining charms her with nonstop small talk, name-dropping, and gossip about the rich and famous, intentionally avoiding discussion of the magazine altogether. George Wren marvels at this performance ("It was, George supposed, like watching your opponent run off a hundred balls at pool").

Having ingratiated himself with the woman, Twining can now disabuse her of the notion that her drama column belongs in *The Outsider*, while at the same time suggesting that Tyler has used her for his purposes:

> "You're no good at that kind of thing, you know," Twining said gently, fondly. "I could tell you you were, of course, but you wouldn't really respect me for that, would you? I'm in the magazine business, not in the flattery business. You know as well as I do that people with money are seldom told the truth. Many so-called friends encourage them to make fools of themselves. (*OP*, 221)

Twining thus reestablishes order on his own terms, though the labor involved in chastising, cajoling, outflanking, and otherwise quelling his employees' uncivil behavior toward him and toward one another has drained him. In Wilfred Sheed's world, interpersonal conflicts are a fact of life. The real work of the organization, it would seem, gets done not because of but *in spite of* the people collectively responsible for doing it. Effective leadership depends as much on a mastery of office politics as it does on professional expertise.

The Fallacy of "Managing with Heart"

I thought about Sheed's characters while reading a best-selling book published in 1995 called *Emotional Intelli-*

gence, by Daniel Goleman, a noted psychologist.[3] Goleman's work, reissued in paperback in 1997, is one of a current spate of books that attempts to rekindle concern for human relationships in business in the wake of painful downsizing in most industries. His overall thesis is that managing people successfully requires the development of our emotional as well as mental resources. Self-understanding as well as a recognition of the impulses that truly motivate people call to a great extent on what Goleman calls "emotional IQ."

Goleman's chapter on the uses of a high emotional IQ in business management is called "Managing with Heart." As this title implies, the author's position is that there are measurable benefits to an organization's managers'

> being skilled in the basic emotional competencies—
> being attuned to the feelings of those we deal with, being
> able to handle conflicts so that they do not escalate. . . .
> Leadership is not domination, but the art of persuading
> people to work toward a common goal. (*EI*, 149)

Goleman finds the opinion of a fellow psychologist instructive in this regard:

> There was a long period of managerial domination of the
> corporate hierarchy when the manipulative, jungle-fighter
> boss was rewarded. But that rigid hierarchy started break-
> ing down in the 1980s under the twin pressures of global-
> ization and information technology. The jungle fighter
> symbolizes where the corporation has been; the virtuoso in
> interpersonal skills is the corporate future. (*EI*, 149)

I am not at all sure why doing business globally in the information age requires a radically new style of leadership, or for that matter only *one* style of leadership. I know plenty of old-style jungle fighters and martinets running highly profitable operations. I also know that "interpersonal skills" were as valuable in the past and are as valuable in the present as they purportedly will be in the "corporate future."

With Wilfred Sheed's wily chief editor in mind, I find myself going only halfway with Goleman. In the sense that Gilbert Twining is "attuned to the feelings of his staff," he possesses one of Goleman's prerequisites for leadership. That leadership is "not domination," however, is questionable. In his own genteel way, Twining is a practiced "jungle-fighter," and it is not by persuasion, but only by manipulation and by the leveraging of his "personal ascendancy" that he is able to counteract disorder at his office.

My point here is that Goleman's argument for "emotionally intelligent" leadership is simplistic. There are obviously situations that require managing "with heart," or by reference to a "common goal." Wilfred Sheed's fictional scenario convinces me, though, that the "proper" way to handle interpersonal conflict in real life is to adapt your approach to the individuals, circumstances, and emotional issues at stake.

It seems to me that Sheed has got it right. Managers and executives who take a flexible approach to myriad interpersonal conflicts are more adept at dealing with them than those who always deal with diverse problems in the same way. There were times in my own career as a senior executive when I felt like a character actor, called on to assume a variety of different roles.

I have always been more comfortable with the classic—OK, conventional—method of managing conflict: "listen hard," "keep your emotions in check," "track the conflict to its source," and so on. Being sweetly reasonable, though, never got me very far with an overbearing executive. People like this exert a disproportionate influence at group meetings. They operate largely by cowing others, and I found that I could handle them to advantage only by giving them a dollop of their own medicine. Now this sometimes meant matching expletive for expletive. This tactic works best if used sparingly; overused, it loses its shock value. Goleman's recipe, "Managing with Heart," is palatable, but it is sometimes more effective when seasoned with pepper.

Some years ago, I was asked to give a speech at the retirement party of a 50-year veteran of our firm, someone I admired (no doubt because his temperament and management style were similar to my own). I noted, and nodding heads confirmed, that I had never heard him raise his voice to an employee or colleague in a dispute. On reflection, I'm not at all sure that's always a virtue. One thing I do know: If you choose to act "out of character," you have to pick your moment carefully. An emotional IQ helps.

Likewise, there were special times when I felt I had to cut off discussion altogether and abandon my preferred collegial manner of trying to find an acceptable compromise among warring parties within the company. National consumer advertising of the Maidenform brand was one of the areas that fell naturally into the category of irreconcilable conflict and had to be handled accordingly. This is one subject about which *everyone* has an opinion—and a strong opinion at that. Unlike inventory control, say, brand advertising does not readily lend itself to analysis based on hard data. Ask sales managers and they'll tell you that national consumer advertising means nothing to the retailer in Peoria and never pushes goods through the stores the way cooperative newspaper advertising with retailers does. Financial executives fail to envision any return on what they regard as an outsized investment, since the results of national advertising are so hard to measure. And operations executives combine the thinking of sales and finance.

These points of view can hardly surprise anyone. What is irksome, though, is how hostility toward national advertising can so easily turn into a personal issue. No amount of patience on my part in alerting executives to the competitive advantages of our national advertising could ever produce a consensus or even a rapprochement among them. Despite my predilection for reasoning things through, I realized quickly enough that there are some things that can be decided only by cutting off debate. This was one issue on which I felt I had to manage by fiat in the interest of redirecting executive energies to other, equally pressing company matters.

My point here is that no one management style is inherently better than another. The more we impose our preferred management style on situations that require us to act "out of character," the less effective, I believe, we are bound to be as executives. Flexibility is primary. Ranking tennis players, I've noticed, usually size up their opponents' style of play and adjust their games accordingly rather than stick to a single favored strategy that may be effective against some players, but not others. They have an assortment of strokes that they use to advantage: lobs, dinks, smashes, slices, over-spins, and the like. Knowing their opponents' strengths and weaknesses, they vary their pace and keep their opponents guessing. Sometimes they adopt baseline, sometimes serve-and-volley, tactics, as needed. That's the way they control the game. And that's the way a flexible manager stays in control, too.

Out of Control: James Thurber's "The Catbird Seat"

The fictions of business also testify to the *disorder* that can result when a chief executive forfeits control of his business and lets interpersonal conflicts fester. James Thurber's short story, "The Catbird Seat," is a counterpart to *Office Politics* on this point.[4] Written in 1945, Thurber's comic tale has been anthologized as frequently as his famous story, "The Secret Life of Walter Mitty." Each story depicts a self-effacing man, who, when his forbearance is sorely tried, creates a new, more aggressive character for himself. The difference is that Walter Mitty reinvents himself only in his imagination. Erwin Martin, the meek hero of "The Catbird Seat," does so in a real-life corporate setting.

The besetting problem for the unprepossessing Martin, loyal head of the filing department for F&S, is that his company president, Mr. Fitweiler, has made an "error" that, after due consideration, Martin feels he must "correct." Fitweiler has hired a self-styled efficiency expert, Mrs. Ulgine Barrows, as his personal assistant. Apparently, she had insinuated herself at a cocktail party into the good graces of the venerable—and vulnerable—Fitweiler. Subsequently, he gave her carte blanche to make wholesale changes in the organization. For two years going, she has terrorized the office staff.

To Martin this corporate predator, with her "quacking voice and braying laugh" is an "obscene woman," who stands "charged with willful, blatant, and persistent attempts to destroy the efficiency and system of F&S." It is clear to him that his own department is threatened by upheaval at the hands of Mrs. Barrows.

> She had, for almost two years now, baited him. In the halls, in the elevator, even in his own office, into which she romped now and then like a circus horse, she was constantly shouting these silly questions at him. "Are you lifting the oxcart out of the ditch? Are you tearing up the pea patch? . . . Are you sitting in the catbird seat?" (CS, 636)

One of Martin's assistants has explained to him that "sitting in the catbird seat" means "sitting pretty, like a batter with three balls and no strikes on him." Martin's patience is at an end.

Martin's single-handed scheme to restore order by contriving to "rub out" Mrs. Barrows looks pretty good on paper, but is doomed to failure simply because he is pathetically inept at plotting murder. He plans to stop in, uninvited, on Mrs. Barrows at her home, stab her the first chance he gets with whatever sharp object he happens to find on hand, then contrive to mislead the police by leaving a cigarette butt in the ashtray (he is known to be a nonsmoker). But once in her house, his plan fizzles when he is unable to find an appropriate murder weapon.

Ironically, however, the moment of his failure sparks his great inspiration. In the company of his nemesis, the meek, unassuming Martin contrives to act completely out of character, smoking, drinking, and vowing to prepare a bomb "which, he confides to Mrs. Barrows, will blow the old goat [Mr. Fitweiler] higher than hell." Shocked at his behavior, Mrs. Barrows throws him out.

> "I'm sitting in the catbird seat," he said. He stuck his tongue out at her and left. Nobody saw him go. (CS, 641)

Once again his normal retiring self at the office the next day, Martin is called upon by Mr. Fitweiler to answer the accusations of an outraged Mrs. Barrows. Predictably, he registers shock and bewilderment. The boss concludes that, given Martin's untarnished reputation for probity, modesty, and discretion, his accuser, Mrs. Barrows, must be suffering from paranoia and hallucinations and, therefore, must be dismissed. In the course of this conversation, Martin finds out that his act of revenge was very well timed indeed:

> "You may not know, Martin, but Mrs. Barrows had planned a reorganization of your department—subject to my approval, of course, subject to my approval. This brought you, rather than anyone else, to her mind. . . . (CS, 643)

The story's payoff is one that anybody forced to put up with the arrogance of a Mrs. Barrows would relish:

[Mrs. Barrows] brayed loudly and hysterically, and the fury was on her again. She glared at Mr. Fitweiler. "Can't you see how he has tricked us, you old fool? Can't you see his little game?" But Mr. Fitweiler had been surreptitiously pressing all the buttons under the top of his desk and employees of F&S began pouring into the room. . . . Stockton, who had played a little football in high school, blocked Mrs. Barrows as she made for Mr. Martin. It took him and Fishbein together to force her out of the door into the hall. . . . (CS, 643)

How true to life—and death—"The Catbird Seat" remains today. If you have ever suffered someone else's incivility, let alone self-aggrandizement, over a long period, you can appreciate how ill-will and resentment can build unnoticed within a decorous and routinized environment. Even the meek and unassuming have their limits. There are few things more vivid in my memory of years at a corporate office than the sudden eruption of a secretary with an otherwise pliant disposition at an executive whose abrasive manner invariably made trivial things seem like very large ones.

The executive, a senior vice president, was one of those short-tempered individuals who rankle you without realizing it. He had obviously grown into the habit of taking people for granted, especially the people who reported to him. That, and the fact that his tone of voice never varied, so that the simplest request—for a Xerox copy, for a phone number— sounded like a peremptory demand. One day I saw his long-time secretary rise from her desk with her steno pad in hand; she appeared to be about to walk into this executive's office, adjacent to mine, to take dictation. Instead, she stood stock-still and, with reddening face, glared at him, letting forth with a stream of invective, beginning (mildly) with "Who the hell do you think you're talking to, Mr. X . . ." and building from there.

The incident, which lasted no more than a minute or two, was startling precisely because it seemed to arise out of the blue. I suspect that her outburst was attributable less to *what* it was that the executive asked of her than to *how* he asked it. It was clear, in any case, that this was the proverbial last straw. She was really reacting to years of accumulated resentment, the force of which came welling up in tears of rage and recrimination.

The executive himself was nonplused. Since his abrupt manner was habitual with him, how could he appreciate the grating effect he had on her, whatever it was that he had requested? The secretary, for her part, had simply accepted each directive from him with little fuss, although obviously with mounting resentment. Once she had vented her anger, of course, she quickly reverted to her customary manner. I don't know what feelings each subsequently harbored, though I can guess. Suffice it to say that the executive was somewhat less overbearing and the secretary somewhat less diffident after that. Though the incident was short-lived, I remember it as if it happened yesterday. If a suitable murder weapon had been handy at the point of eruption, I don't think I'd have bet on her not to use it.

Nowadays, especially, with so much stress in the workplace, both for those whose jobs are being outsourced or phased out and for those who have to work doubly hard to keep them, Thurber's story about the lengths an individual will go to when threatened, as Mr. Martin was, with imminent "reorganization," is revealing. Today's human resource experts counsel us to be vigilant about inconsistent behavior on the part of employees, yet people like Martin are often impossible to read under such circumstances. His revenge is sweet precisely because he is perceived to be unvarying in his behavior. Further, Martin's method of "rubbing out" Ulgine Barrows happens in a way that Martin *himself* is least able to predict!

I have no doubt that Thurber, were he alive today, would find some of today's workplace stories of bizarre confrontations and irreconcilable conflicts all too familiar, predictable in their unpredictability. Conversely, I suspect that the company president who thought the 56-year-old woman harmless might have spared himself the agony of her retribution if he had read "The Catbird Seat."

Managing Situations of Extreme Stress: Joseph Conrad's "Typhoon"

Sheed and Thurber's satires of untoward behavior in business remind us of how easily order and civility can be undermined. For me, though, Joseph Conrad's story, "Typhoon," offers the most probing example of what really matters to men under extreme stress, when chaos threatens order and tries your personal values as a leader.

Conrad's tale, written in 1901, is one of the most stirring stories of survival at sea ever written.[5] The author himself went to sea as a first mate aboard a ship plying the South China Sea similar to the one he describes in his story. His tale, therefore, has an extraordinary authenticity. What makes "Typhoon" a singular adventure, though, is Conrad's exploration of character, how individuals in a chain of command variously react when the world seems to be caving in on them—literally. At a time when articles and books on what will be required of organizations, teams, and leaders in the twenty-first century are proliferating, Conrad's early-twentieth-century story provides some unique guidance to crisis management.

The sequence of events in "Typhoon" is simple. The *Nan-Shan*, a steamer with an English crew, is carrying some cargo as well as two hundred Chinese laborers to their homes on the mainland of China from "various tropical colonies," where they have just completed a few years of labor. The captain of the *Nan-Shan*, a man named MacWhirr, observes a sharply falling barometer, a sure sign, as he says, that there is "some dirty weather knocking about." He and his crew gird for a storm.

After deciding not to skirt the oncoming storm but to confront it head-on, MacWhirr presently finds his ship being battered by a typhoon so fierce and unrelenting that at one point he alone believes she has a chance of pulling through. It is up to this courageous man not simply to guide the ship through the tempest, but to keep his demoralized crew functional. To make matters worse, he learns that the Chinese in the lower deck are fighting desperately among themselves to recover their money and possessions that the violence of the typhoon has shaken loose from their trunks and strewn about the deck. At the very height of the storm, MacWhirr insists that his crew go below to quell the riot. Then, against all odds, the captain leads the *Nan-Shan* through the rest of the typhoon.

"Typhoon" would be a great story by virtue alone of Conrad's realistic description of the storm and survival at sea. Its chief interest, however, lies in its equally realistic depiction of the stresses on human character that the storm induces. Captain MacWhirr is not simply another heroic figure who summons the courage to withstand a severe crisis. In fact, our principal interest in this man is that he is a decidedly nonheroic figure.

Conrad shows MacWhirr from the beginning of the story to be a most improbable captain. He is ordinary-looking, stolid, and unimaginative. Yet these are precisely the qualities that allow him to keep his composure during the storm and to concentrate single-mindedly on the job at hand. His key officers are smarter than he and harbor a mild contempt for what they consider his simple-mindedness. None, however, possesses his passion for order. This last quality may seem irrelevant to negotiating a monster typhoon in the South China Sea, but Conrad shows it to be essential at the very moment when the storm threatens the ship most severely.

It is precisely at this critical juncture that the boatswain informs Captain MacWhirr about the commotion in the deck below, where the Chinese are pummeling each other for the gold coins they have lost and being pummeled themselves by the typhoon.

> "All them Chinamen in the fore tween-deck have fetched away, sir. . . . In a lump . . . seen them myself. . . . Awful sight, sir . . . thought . . . tell you." (T, 74)

At the most improbable moment, when he himself is almost washed overboard by the storm, MacWhirr orders Jukes, his first mate, to go down to the "tween deck" to see if he can settle the dispute. The order must be carried out, of course, but the first mate is struck dumb. How can the captain be thinking of the Chinese laborers when the crew itself is at mortal risk, and he needs every good hand he can get to see the ship through the typhoon?

> What the devil did the coolies matter to anybody? . . . the extremity of the ship made what went on inside of her appear of little moment. . . .

> "What am I to do then, sir?" And the trembling of his whole wet body caused Jukes' voice to sound like bleating. . . .

> The absurdity of the demand made upon him revolted Jukes. He was as unwilling to go as if the moment he had left the deck the ship were sure to sink. (*T*, 80–81)

MacWhirr's command comes at a point when the rest of the crew is not only demoralized, but made insensible to anything but their own immediate safety. The ferocity of the typhoon has induced a crippling fatalism in the men. None sees any hope of survival. MacWhirr nonetheless prevails. He will not be defied, whereupon the crew, now goaded into concerted action, contrives to form a cordon around the rioting Chinese and collect the gold coins. Though fearful that the Chinese will misunderstand their intention and turn their wrath against them, the crew members thus prevent further rioting.

Still resentful at having been ordered to perform what he calls an absurd and "odious" task, Jukes afterward reminds the captain that the Chinese could not have known that the crew was there to restore order, not to "plunder them." MacWhirr's reply is laconic, but telling: "had to do what's fair." A little while later, the first mate, still smoldering, confronts him again, whereupon the captain, with unaccustomed vehemence, elaborates on his motive:

> Had to do what's fair, for all—they are only Chinamen. Give them the same chance with ourselves—hang it all. She isn't lost yet. Bad enough to be shut up below in a gale— . . . —without being battered to pieces. . . . Couldn't let that go on in my ship, if I knew she hadn't five minutes to live. Couldn't bear it, Mr. Jukes. (*T*, 102)

Implicit in these words is a sense of ethical responsibility powerful enough to transcend even the sense of impending physical calamity. For MacWhirr, the sense of fairness is instinctive, part of the captain's very being. His sense of fairness is also inseparable from his passion for order. Conrad vividly conveys the exceptional qualities of an unexceptional man by making us privy to his solitary reflection on the incident in light of his knowledge that the worst of the storm is yet to come:

> He was glad the trouble in the tween-deck had been discovered in time. If the ship had to go after all, then, at least, she wouldn't be going to the bottom with a lot of people in her fighting teeth and claw. That would have been odious. And in that feeling there was a humane intention and a vague sense of the fitness of things. (*T*, 100)

However vividly Conrad describes the storm, he is not out to generate a superficial suspense so much as to underscore the moral as well as physical courage of the *Nan-Shan's* captain. As the author says, MacWhirr's actions partake "of the nature of the man."

Now we have come very far indeed from the uncalamitous, landlubbing world of business management. Or have we? It is clear that Conrad is using the sea setting simply as a backdrop to the study of character. What interests him as a writer are the principles, attitudes, and ideas—in short, the values—that drive individuals to make choices and judgments under conditions of extreme stress.

In the depiction of his central character, Captain Mac-Whirr, Conrad reveals how a leader's values relate to the management of conflict. Management textbooks see as axiomatic the need to manage rather than to avoid conflict wherever possible. The lead article in a recent newsletter from the Harvard Business School carries the title, "Don't Avoid Conflicts—Manage Them." The gist of the article is that managers who take the expedient way out and ignore conflict ultimately pay an unacceptable price in the loss of productivity and the loss of focus on the task at hand. Better to deal with conflict directly by trying to understand "how others are likely to react, and why."[6]

Similarly, Joseph Conrad's CEO, Captain MacWhirr, embodies the general principle that an executive should manage rather than avoid conflict. Yet good sense argues *against* his doing so. Surely marshaling his men to help combat the dire external threat to the ship takes precedence over diverting his resources to settle the dispute among his passengers. In the extremity of the moment, there are no practical benefits to what he does, only downsides. Conrad makes it clear to the reader that MacWhirr could have ignored the conflict below decks with impunity and, furthermore, that his choice, by any standard, jeopardizes his ship and crew. What is it, then, that for MacWhirr overrides these considerations?

MacWhirr's actions derive solely from who he is—in other words, from his most deeply held values as an individual. Everything he does, even going down with his ship, must make sense *in terms of* those values, those core beliefs. Put another way, the captain's actions are rooted in what Conrad aptly calls a "humane intention." The idea of people "fighting teeth and claw" is odious to MacWhirr because it is uncivilized, contrary to the human impulse for order, and to the captain's "sense of the fitness of things." It is what he owes the Chinese as fellow human beings that matters—*all* that matters at that moment.

There is no operating manual that can inculcate these values or, least of all, tell how to apply them in particular circumstances. At several points in the book, Conrad's hero declares to his resentful first mate that "you can't find everything in books." When the time comes, MacWhirr ignores prepackaged wisdom and draws on the values that partake "of his nature." Supreme among these is the categorical imperative of order at all costs. In terms of conventional management theory, MacWhirr seems perverse. He insists on managing conflict, but for all the wrong reasons. His actions are neither "productive" nor "focused" on the chief order of business: surviving the typhoon. All he has to go by is an unalterable inner directive.

The hero of Conrad's novel is a most unprepossessing man. His self-effacing, undemonstrative nature runs contrary to the stereotypical image of the imposing, take-charge chief executive officer. By representing him as a colorless man who disappoints our expectations, Conrad underscores the importance of those inner characteristics that "image" alone cannot convey, but that emerge when untoward circumstances call them forth.

Real-World Management Under Duress: Climbing Mt. Everest

For extreme situations, Conrad's "off the charts" storm would seem to defy real-world comparisons. If anything, though, the storm at the summit of Mt. Everest that claimed 12 lives in a 1996 climbing expedition, runs a close second. According to one of the survivors, Jon Krakauer, in his best-selling book *Into Thin Air,* "attempting to climb Everest is an intrinsically irrational act—a triumph of desire over sensibility."[7] To attempt the climb, in other words, is deliberately to flirt with disaster. There is not only the risk of violent, unpredictable storms, but also the risk of people literally losing their minds at the upper altitudes, where the lack of oxygen often causes severe disorientation, impaired judgment, and, if not treated promptly, permanent brain damage and death.

These conditions make the quality of leadership critical. Commissioned by *Outside* magazine to write a first-hand account of the climb, Krakauer asks a good question in recalling the disastrous ascent:

> Why did veteran Himalayan guides keep moving upward,
> ushering a gaggle of relatively inexperienced amateurs—
> each of whom had paid as much as $65,000 to be taken
> safely up Everest—into an apparent death trap? (*ITA*, 6)

The way Krakauer phrases the question suggests the answer.
The very nature of the climb as a commercial venture com-
promised some vital strategic decisions on the guides' part at
the very outset. It meant that the climbers were not picked,
as in earlier pioneering days, for their mountaineering experience or teamwork, but for their willingness to fork up huge
fees. For Rob Hall, the famous New Zealand guide who led
Krakauer's group, securing his reputation as a *businessman*
must have been an important priority. Getting as many people to the top as possible apparently took precedence over
his published commitment to ensure the "maximum safety"
of his clients before anything else.

   In fact, there was a double threat to his reputation in
1996. Krakauer notes that Hall had failed to get any of his
clients to the summit the previous year, so the pressure on
him to do so now was especially strong. In addition, he was
in danger of losing his competitive advantage to an American expedition leader who had a "charismatic personality . . . aggressively marketed," and who had scheduled his
climb at the same time as Hall's.

> Under the circumstances, the prospect of turning his
> clients around while his rival's clients were pushing
> toward the summit may have been sufficiently distasteful
> to cloud Hall's judgment. (*ITA*, 273)

Even before undertaking the climb, though, Hall, who was also one of the casualties, seems to have ignored some of the cardinal rules of climbing that he himself had been careful to impress on his group of amateurs before the ascent. That *business* considerations may well have been uppermost in Hall's mind is evident in his encouragement of his clients to attempt to reach the summit without allowing sufficient time to descend safely before dark.

Krakauer pointedly notes Hall's insistence that his group follow his every command as leader on summit day. The guide insisted that the climbers stay within 100 meters of each other, so that he and his assistant guide could monitor them. He also knew that starting *down* from the summit after two in the afternoon would put the climbers at an unacceptable risk. Yet the group became strung out before long; and while three members of the group had the good sense voluntarily to withdraw from the summit attempt on the final day when they knew they couldn't make it, Hall was determined to see to it that the rest of the group made the summit, especially a repeat customer who had been forced to turn back only 300 feet from the summit the year before. He made it this time, but died in the descent because Hall ignored his own timetable for getting his clients up and *down* safely.

Krakauer tries to mitigate Hall's responsibility for such risk taking by reminding us that "lucid thought is all but impossible at 29,000 feet." But isn't this precisely the reason for adhering to sound mountaineering principles in the first place? I find it gruesomely symbolic of his failure to follow his own dictates that the leader of this expedition died alone, isolated on the upper reaches of the mountain. That Hall met with a violent but by no means unusual storm that caused several deaths is not a matter of bad luck so much as bad judgment.

As autocrats in their respective realms of sea and mountain, MacWhirr and Hall are similar in that they both faced life-or-death decisions under extreme conditions. As leaders, though, they stand at polar extremes. MacWhirr adheres to his principles, which have a profoundly human basis. By so doing, he reasserts human order in the very midst of nature's chaos. Hall compromises his principles when it seems advantageous. He disregards his own mandate for tight team discipline and thereby invites disaster.

Krakauer speculates that disaster would have been avoided if the storm had come an hour earlier or two hours later than it did. I find such speculation meaningless. The real issue is one of leadership and of the principles that a good leader needs—and needs to *act* on—in a critical situation. It is by his adherence to human priorities that MacWhirr maximizes the teamwork of his crew. It is by his neglect of those same priorities that Hall forfeits any advantage that an orderly procedure might have afforded him.

Maintaining Order Through Consensus Management

Interestingly, the businesspeople Captain MacWhirr puts me most in mind of are the Japanese. The passion for order in their affairs is as deeply embedded in the Japanese character as it is in MacWhirr's. And their discipline in enforcing order as their first priority is no less stringent than his. During my visits to Japan on business, I noticed that the Japanese do not react to disorderly or uncivil behavior. Just as MacWhirr insists on averting chaos below decks during the typhoon by ordering his crew to contain the rioting, so the Japanese preempt disorder by observing a preset ritual at business meetings and by cultivating social relationships outside the office.

Some years ago I was involved in a round-table discussion with Japanese executives from the trading company that represented Maidenform there. The issues regarding the marketing and distribution of our brand in Japan were complex and subject to widely different points of view. As though by prearrangement, we presented our views first. The head of the Japanese office took up our points one by one with his managers, letting each person voice his approval or objection. Alternatives and modifications to our plan were suggested periodically and were adopted only when everyone at the conference table had signalled his agreement.

This process, I realized, was what consensus management, so called, was all about. There must have been sharp disagreements, yet they were always kept under control by the ritualistic manner of discussion. I will admit to a preference for short meetings as a rule, so my patience at what, by my standards, seemed an excruciatingly prolonged session, frayed badly. Indeed, it was hard for an unaccustomed Westerner to know who was in agreement and who wasn't at any given point, since the meeting was so decorous and formal.

The formality of all this belied the importance the Japanese place on cultivating good personal relationships. The next day, the three Japanese executives invited me out for a day of golf at a country club outside Tokyo. At the end of the round, while our foursome soaked serenely in the clubhouse hot tub, the senior executive told me something that I have never forgotten: "You know, Mr. Brawer, one day on the golf course is worth five years in the conference room." And it occurred to me then, as it occurs to me now, that Japanese businessmen do not manage conflict so much as preempt it. How much weight the Japanese give to cultivating mutual trust as the basis for long-term business relationships. It isn't hard to understand why they are among the least litigious people, especially when compared to Americans.

This is by no means to say that we should—or can— emulate the Japanese. Granted, operating by consensus has its advantages. Yet Americans are far too individualistic and independent-minded to tolerate meetings of the kind I have described. The great challenge is to recognize that interpersonal conflicts come with the territory, that they are often hard to separate from business matters, and that, as executives, we have to do what we can to contain them to maintain order in the workplace.

The fictions of business show us how complex that task can be, yet how necessary it is. Writers take a dark—and I think realistic—view of interpersonal conflict. They make us conscious of human fallibility and vagaries of conduct— our own and others'—precisely at those moments when we would prefer to get on with business and let interpersonal problems solve themselves. They recognize that the job of containing (not resolving) interpersonal conflicts depends, not on textbook solutions, but on ad hoc ingenuity and flexibility. There are no all-purpose paradigms for managers as to how to preempt or minimize conflict, no one-size-fits-all solution. The leader's job is to recognize that interpersonal conflict is one of the things in a world of change that never changes; that handling disputes, whether overt or unspoken, is as integral to your job as meeting project deadlines; that each case has its own causes and its own peculiarities and must be handled accordingly; and that your own *personal* values are the ultimate breakwater against typhoon-force conflicts in corporate life.

CONCLUSION:
THE MORE THINGS
CHANGE . . .

I n a business world where everyone agrees that managing an ever accelerating rate of change requires looking forward, not back, what important insights can the fictions of business offer executives and managers? How to increase productivity? How to build a competitive advantage? How to process information more efficiently? How to compete abroad? How to merge and acquire? Assuredly *not*. In fact, the plays and novels I have discussed in this book serve a different but no less important function. They sensitize us to those peculiarly human issues in the workplace that are impervious to change and that we cannot ignore because they test and challenge us every day of our working lives.

Great literature keeps us honest. Writers like George Bernard Shaw, Sinclair Lewis, and Mark Twain sensitize us to the myopia that often afflicts us and caution us not to take ourselves and our roles too seriously. Joseph Heller and Anthony Trollope remind us that the orderly, rational universe we, as managers, would like to believe in does not exist. Their novels depict a world of illusion and appearance that both sustains and confounds us. Arthur Miller, Wilfred

Sheed, and Joseph Conrad remind us that individual and collective self-delusion, the struggle for power and control in corporate hierarchies, and the conflicting claims of personal and organizational values pervade our lives as businesspeople. These are the kinds of issues that do not go away by themselves. Nor can they be shunted off to Human Resources. They are problems that will recur even in the best of times, and changes in the way we do business will not mitigate them. Unattended to, they can derail our business strategies. They therefore require our ongoing personal attention.

For me, the signal benefit of the fictions of business is that they activate the all-important process of self-scrutiny. I say "all-important" because we pride ourselves on our ability to typecast the people we manage, while at the same time erecting all sorts of screens against looking at ourselves as our colleagues and staff do. In fact, I have often observed that managers sometimes embody the very shortcomings or deficiencies that they attribute to the people they manage. The dilemmas of Willy Loman, Charles Gray, George Babbitt, and Bob Slocum belong, strictly speaking, only to the realm of fiction, yet their faltering efforts at self-recognition are of universal concern. In them, we see how the personal tensions between self-deception and understanding, egotism and generosity, vulnerability and strength of character variously play out in a business setting. Characters as disparate in personality and temperament as Tom Rath, Andrew Undershaft, and Captain MacWhirr all demonstrate in their words and acts the need for *self*-management as a priority in managing an organization.

Taken together, the novels and plays just discussed comprise an inventory of our inner resources, first as *individuals* and then as managers. One of their chief virtues as literature is that they put us in touch with ourselves. For it is only through *self*-definition that we can begin to understand the complex motives and often contradictory impulses that drive the people we manage. The fictions of business prompt us to examine and to reexamine the values, biases, and preconceptions that underlie the tasks we undertake as professional managers. Because great literature reflects familiar patterns of behavior in a variety of circumstances, it reinforces an old adage: The more things change, the more they remain the same.

The fictions of business give us the undreamed of competitive advantage of 20/20 hindsight. They are liberating. They free us from our conventional assumptions about the people we manage and from the fictions we harbor about ourselves. At their best, they tell us what we may not want to hear, but what we most need to know. Unlike self-help, inspirational, and how-to manuals, they dispense no advice; they preach no morals; they prescribe no rules. In a world of great change, the fictions of business offer us vivid testimony as to what remains constant in human nature and in human affairs.

NOTES

CHAPTER ONE

1. Quoted in William Leach, *Land of Desire* (New York: Random House, 1993), 76.
2. Theodore Dreiser, *Sister Carrie* (New York: Limited Editions Club, 1939), 17–18.
3. 13 July, 1997.
4. David Mamet, *Glengarry Glen Ross* (New York: Grove Press, 1984). Cited in text as GGR.
5. Stephen R. Covey, *The Seven Habits of Highly Effective People* (New York: Simon and Schuster, 1989).

CHAPTER TWO

1. *Wall Street Journal*, 3 Sept. 1997.
2. *New York Times*, 16 Dec. 1996.
3. *New Yorker*, 26 Jan. 1998.
4. Horatio Alger, Jr., *Ragged Dick and Struggling Upward* (New York: Penguin Books, 1986). Cited in text as RD.
5. *Chaucer's Major Poetry*, ed. Albert C. Baugh (New York: Appleton Century Crofts, 1963), 243–244. Translation mine.
6. Anthony Trollope, *The Way We Live Now* (New York: Oxford University Press, 1991), 34. Cited in text as WLN.

7. John Rothchild, *Going for Broke* (New York: Simon and Schuster, 1991).

8. Rothchild, 20.

9. *Wall Street Journal*, 16 Sept. 1996.

CHAPTER THREE

1. Sloan Wilson, *The Man in the Grey Flannel Suit* (London: The Reprint Society, 1957). Cited in text as MS.

2. Arthur Miller, *Timebends: A Life* (New York: Grove, 1987), 191.

3. Arthur Miller, *Death of a Salesman* (New York: Viking, 1958). Cited in text as DS.

4. John P. Marquand, *Point of No Return* (Boston: Little, Brown, 1949). Cited in text as PNR.

5. Mihaly Csikszentmihalyi, *Flow: The Psychology of Optimal Experience* (New York: Harper and Row, 1991). See esp. Chapter 7, "Work as Flow."

6. From a speech given by Zalman C. Bernstein at the Second Annual Bernstein Pension Conference, Sept. 17, 1984.

CHAPTER FOUR

1. Joseph Heller, *Something Happened* (New York: Dell, 1989). Cited in text as SH.

2. Michael Hammer and James Champy, *Reengineering the Corporation* (New York: HarperCollins; 1993).

3. *The Downsizing of America* (New York: Times Books, 1996). Cited in text as DA.

4. 13 Jan. 1995.

5. 14 May 1996.

6. Michael Hammer and Steven A. Stanton, *The Reengineering*

Revolution (New York: HarperCollins, 1995). Cited in text as *RR*.

7. George Bernard Shaw, *Complete Plays and Prefaces* (New York: Dodd, Mead, 1962), 1: 299–466. Cited in text as *MB*.

CHAPTER FIVE

1. *New York Times*, 16 Dec. 1996.
2. *Time*, 13 Jan. 1997.
3. *Wall Street Journal*, 9 Oct. 1996.
4. Theodore Dreiser, *The Financier* (New York: Penguin, Meridian Classic, 1986). Cited in text as *F*.
5. James B. Stewart, *Den of Thieves* (New York: Simon and Schuster, 1991). Cited in text as *DT*.
6. Daniel Fischel, *Payback: The Conspiracy to Destroy Michael Milken and His Financial Revolution* (New York: HarperBusiness, 1995).
7. *Wall Street Journal*, 15 July 1996.
8. *Wall Street Journal*, 4 Feb. 1997.
9. Sinclair Lewis, *Babbitt* (New York: Harcourt Brace, 1950). Cited in text as *B*.
10. *New Yorker*, 16 Mar. 1997.
11. Alfred P. Sloan, *My Years With General Motors* (New York: Currency Doubleday, 1990). Cited in text as *GM*.
12. Daniel J. Boorstin, *The Americans: The Democratic Experience* (New York: Vintage Books, 1974), 368–369.
13. *Harvard Business Review*, Mar.–Apr. 1997:12.
14. John Dos Passos, *U.S.A.* (New York: Random House, Modern Library, 1937). Cited in text as *TBM*.
15. Quoted in James C. Collins and Jerry I. Porras, *Built to Last* (New York: HarperBusiness, 1994), 57.
16. Quoted in Collins, 56.

17. Upton Sinclair, *The Jungle* (New York: Penguin Classics, 1986). Cited in text as *J.*
18. *Wall Street Journal,* 1 Dec. 1994.
19. Mark Twain, *A Connecticut Yankee in King Arthur's Court* (New York: Signet Classics, n.d.). Cited in text as CY.

CHAPTER SIX

1. 16 Oct. 1996.
2. Wilfred Sheed, *Office Politics* (New York: Simon and Schuster, Pocket Books, 1968). Cited in text as OP.
3. Daniel Goleman, *Emotional Intelligence* (New York: Bantam Books, Bantam Trade Paperbacks, 1997). Cited in text as *EI.*
4. James Thurber, "The Catbird Seat," in *James Thurber: Writings and Drawings,* ed. Garrison Keillor (New York: Penguin Books, The Library of America, 1996). Cited in text as CS.
5. Joseph Conrad, "Typhoon," in *Joseph Conrad: Three Tales of the Sea* (Los Angeles: The Limited Editions Club, 1972). Cited in text as *T.*
6. Monci J. Williams, "Don't Avoid Conflicts—Manage Them," *Management Update, Harvard Business School* 2 (July 1997): 3.
7. Jon Krakauer, *Into Thin Air* (New York: Villard, 1997). Cited in text as *ITA.*

A WORKING MAN AND WOMAN'S GUIDE TO FURTHER READING

I have listed below those books that have stimulated my thinking about the human problems and issues in corporate life, *and* that have been fun to read. Some of these works deal with issues I have not taken up here, or have only touched on incidentally. The novels and plays marked with an asterisk are discussed in the preceding chapters. I hope these focused discussions will encourage people to read the works in full and to explore on their own the fictions of business. I have always held that writers of fiction have no automatic claim to our attention. They should give us good reason to set aside precious nonworking hours for reading their works. My own rule of thumb when reading a novel or play is this: If it is not *enjoyable*, put it down and move on.

*The Canterbury Tales, by Geoffrey Chaucer

Chaucer's fourteenth-century world is one in which mercantile values are pervasive. Only the most spiritual and self-effacing abjure them, and these individuals seem to belong to another world. The language of commerce, the acquisitive impulse, and the profit motive characterize a broad cross-section of Chaucer's pilgrims, from merchant to friar, from prioress to guildsman, from canon's yeoman to pardoner, from physician to the oft-wed wife of Bath. The poet himself was the son of a merchant and knew well how the values of the marketplace drive the world.

*"Typhoon," by Joseph Conrad

Conrad's story celebrates a sea captain's act of rare moral courage during a crisis, with nothing to guide him but his own sense of the "fitness of things." Through his outwardly unimpressive central character, Captain MacWhirr, Conrad demonstrates how moral integrity is a virtue that can often go unrecognized, but that characterizes this true leader as he struggles to rally his crew and to reassert humane values in the midst of nature's chaos.

*The Big Money, by John Dos Passos

Dos Passos was one of the great innovative writers of the first half of the twentieth century. He is hard to categorize because he interweaves fiction, biography, and documentary-style "newsreels" in trying to capture what it takes to succeed in American life. In The Big Money we are witness to the pursuit of the "American dream" of limitless opportunity from the vantage point of everyone from Henry Ford to a nameless vagabond, from idealists to opportunists, from conformists to mavericks. The central conflict in all these stories is a universal one: that between our personal values and the values of a tough, pragmatic, materialistic culture.

The Financier, by Theodore Dreiser

Dreiser's novel, modeled on the life and career of Frank Yerkes, the turn-of-the-century streetcar magnate, is about an ambitious and brilliant businessman who is literally a law unto himself. Flouting convention, public opinion, and received wisdom, Frank Cowperwood forges a financial empire out of guts, brains, and uncompromising self-interest. Dreiser makes it clear that Cowperwood, though clearly set apart from ordinary mortals, ironically embodies every man's unspoken aspirations. The setting of this 1912 novel—a Darwinian world where only the strong survive—is that of our own time and place.

The Last Tycoon, F. Scott Fitzgerald

Fitzgerald did not live to complete his last fiction, but he wrote enough for us to be able to appreciate his acute sense of the mind of the business genius. Monroe Stahr, the central character, is modeled after Irving Thalberg, who became the celebrated head of a major Hollywood movie studio before he was 30. As a business leader, Stahr is nonpareil. Knowing exactly what he wants, he also knows how to get what he wants by playing to the strengths and weaknesses of sensitive screenwriters, headstrong directors, and emotionally deficient actors and actresses. Absolute tyranny is eschewed today in management theory, but Stahr, in his composed way, embodies the virtues of dictatorship in holding a volatile organization together: "Stahr must be right always, not most of the time, but always—or the structure would melt down like gradual butter."

J R, by William Gaddis

Winner of the National Book Award in 1975, Gaddis's comic novel is about an enterprising sixth-grade entrepreneur, who builds an admirably diversified (paper) empire from a mail-order shipment of surplus navy forks. J R, Gaddis's grotesque little hero, has two competitive advantages: first, a thoroughly materialistic mentality uncorrupted by any recognizably human values; second, a circle of grown-up financiers, marketers, and administrators equally committed to self-aggrandizement and ethical irresponsibility. Gaddis may seem cynical to some, but his depiction of how the J R family of companies corners the "education market" anticipates the incursions of today's media tycoons into the public schools in their competition for new, lucrative enterprises.

Something Happened, by Joseph Heller

Heller's novel, a black comedy, takes place in a corporate office where the key executives are color-coded. Green, Black, Brown, and White all engage in a perpetual roundelay of fear and suspicion propagated by the company spin doctor, Bob Slocum. Slocum is a survivor, fine-tuned to the corporate culture. He is expert at producing the kind of data the company needs to maintain the status quo and ensure that no one is unhappy. He is also a past master at telling each executive what he wants to hear and then playing both ends against the middle. Unfortunately, Slocum has lost touch with *himself* in the process. "Who am I?" is the refrain of Slocum's internal dialogues with himself. Beneath his composed exterior, Slocum is an adolescent—insecure, self-doubting, fearful of exposure, and eager to say and do what is expected of him. "I must remember not to smile too much. I must maintain a facade. I must remember to continue acting correctly subservient and clearly grateful. . . ." No contemporary novel that I know reveals so much about the quiet desperation that afflicts the most apparently well-adjusted individuals in corporate life.

Babbitt, by Sinclair Lewis

George Babbitt is a businessman who sacrifices his individuality under the pressure of having to conform to the soul-destroying values of his insular, self-righteous community. Because he lives exclusively for what others deem respectable and socially acceptable, his life is not his own. The more he parrots the gospel of the small-town booster, the more he feels trapped by the politically correct role he has embraced. Babbitt's inchoate longing to please himself—indeed, at one point to "break with everything that was decent and normal"—always gives way to his fear of ostracism. Implicit in Lewis's unsparing satire of small-town

American life is the issue of whether as individuals we make our own choices or whether we are content to have them made for us. This question is particularly pertinent in the corporate world, where compromise between our personal values and those of the company is inevitable.

Nice Work, by David Lodge

Lodge's novel is about the mating of two cultures—in every sense of the word. Vic Wilcox is the manager of an engineering firm in the English Midlands who meets Robyn Penrose, a professor of English, when her car breaks down near his plant. Each, of course, lives in his and her own world, and each, at least at first, is hermetically sealed off from the other temperamentally, attitudinally, and politically. The fun of the novel is seeing the ways in which the two find common ground and lend their special expertise to the solving of each other's business (and emotional) problems. Lodge's premise is identical to my own: The traditional compartmentalization of the humanities and business is nonsensical and mutually impoverishing.

**Glengarry Glen Ross,* by David Mamet

Mamet's play is about the ability of driven salesmen to make you forget who you are and gladly deliver unto them yourself and your newborn. It is also about the desperation of a dog-eat-dog workplace, where the survivors' article of faith is "always be closing." There is no practical guide to the art of salesmanship that shows so unerringly how to make seemingly impossible sales. Mamet's salesmen are sleazy, but in a brutal and brutalizing workplace, they emerge as heroic individuals, the "members of a dying breed."

Point of No Return, by John P. Marquand

Marquand's novel is the story of how Charles Gray, a successful investment banker, goes about trying to liberate himself from a life that seems to him preordained and stereotyped. Feeling trapped inside his "business character," Gray revisits the town where he was raised and reviews his past for clues as to how he has come to be the man he is. The novelist understands his subject well enough to know that a life spent "taking care of other people's money" is not what Gray "had dreamed of"; but that, on the other hand, "if he had to start all over again he would not have acted differently." Self-recognition is an achievement for anyone, and Gray's struggle to attain it is bracing, despite its being tinged with rue.

Bartleby the Scrivener: A Story of Wall Street, by Herman Melville

Melville's short novel is about one of the strangest characters in fiction: a clerk named Bartleby whose polite refusal to do the work he has been hired to do ("I would prefer not to") has a profound and unanticipated effect on his employer and coworkers. The "bond of a common humanity" is what the "eminently safe" lawyer-narrator of this tale comes to see as the link between him and his perverse but always decorous employee. Melville writes passionately about the nameless compulsions that resist conformity to the established routines and conventions of the workplace.

*Death of a Salesman, by Arthur Miller

Miller's famous play is about the terrible consequences of self-betrayal. The world that Willy Loman has fabricated for himself as his shield against reality is literally fantastic, a blend of the comic and the pathetic. He is among the walking dead because he is incapable of self-recognition and, therefore, also incapable of seeing why the world (aside from his wife) shows so little appreciation or understanding of Willy Loman. This is a play to purge us of the self-deceptions, small and large, with which we daily burden and complicate our lives.

*Major Barbara, by George Bernard Shaw

Shaw's play is about a conflict of values between Andrew Undershaft, an arms dealer, and his daughter, Barbara, a major in the Salvation Army. Barbara repudiates what she takes to be her father's crass materialism, while her father scorns the self-justifications of the Army's adherents and indeed of everyone else who does not subscribe to his "one true religion," money. Shaw upends conventional assumptions about what constitutes virtue, as Undershaft proves himself a visionary and benevolent tycoon, and Barbara finds belated salvation in the recognition that she is very much her father's daughter.

Office Politics, by Wilfred Sheed

Sheed's novel is precisely what its title says it's about. Even in an apparently genteel setting like a publishing house, individual ambitions, small and large, invariably assert themselves and, absent strong leadership, roil the organization. For the editor-in-chief, experience in publishing, a clear vision of where he wants to take his weekly magazine, and an eye for great writing are not nearly enough. On the other hand, knowing how to handle a palace revolt while keeping the organization intact is a required skill for Sheed's embattled editor.

The Jungle, by Upton Sinclair

Sinclair's novel, a great international best-seller at the turn of the century, prompted a reform of the notorious meat-packing industry soon after it was published. *The Jungle* is memorable, though, for its harrowing account of how the low-skilled and economically disadvantaged, then and now, have little chance to better themselves, let alone survive, in industries where human dignity and compassion invariably yield to efficiency and self-interest.

*"The Catbird Seat," by James Thurber

Thurber's humorous as well as instructive story is a delicious tale of pure, unadulterated revenge. A plot to murder an executive hellion is narrowly averted, and an even more satisfying form of payback for years of gratuitous remarks and intimidation takes shape in the mind of a meek middle manager incapable of acting out of character, except when threatened with extinction himself.

*The Way We Live Now, by Anthony Trollope

For Trollope, the way his fellow Englishmen and women live occasions only scorn. Trollope's protagonist is an unscrupulous financier who, with a pretense of wealth and respectability, very nearly pulls off a scam of gigantic proportions. Trollope is most convincing and entertaining when he is demonstrating how skillful people are in using and manipulating one another. In this world only those with imagination, aggressiveness, and a lack of scruples need apply. Trollope shows how destructive—and self-destructive—the lust for money and power can be.

*A Connecticut Yankee in King Arthur's Court, by Mark Twain

Twain's hero in this novel is an efficiency expert named Hank Morgan, who finds himself in sixth-century England after accidentally being hit over the head at work. In his efforts to set up modern forms of communication and rid people of their superstitions and ignorance, Hank shows great skill and resourcefulness. Twain is also skillful in exposing us to the ignorance and ultimate self-delusion of inflexible and unenlightened leadership. Who is the real innocent in this story? Who is the ultimate provincial? How quickly we are apt to justify ourselves in the name of technological progress.

Rabbit is Rich, by John Updike

Updike's novel is the third in a series of four about Rabbit Angstrom, a latter-day George Babbitt. As his name implies, Rabbit is in perpetual flight, longing "to break out, to find another self." Updike gets inside his character's skin, so that we come to see and feel Rabbit's unspoken discontent with a life that he finds drab and predictable. As head of a Toyota agency in a medium-sized city in Pennsylvania during the late 1970s, Rabbit is restless and frustrated, struggling to make sense of the second-ratedness of his life and the "deadly staleness" that pervades it. Among other things, the novel is a primer on the emotional pitfalls of accommodating the next generation in a family business.

The Man in the Grey Flannel Suit, by Sloan Wilson

Wilson's hero, Tom Rath, longs for a safe, anonymous corporate existence after the chaos of World War II. He delib-

erately effaces himself trying to chart a course through corporate life that will be safe, comfortable, and devoid of
stress. Self-recognition comes hard to a man whose only
serious reflection is on how best to conform to the organization and to please his boss. Eventually, he rediscovers the
integrity he had lost, but not before circumstances force him
to become his own man.

ACKNOWLEDGMENTS

My chief debt is to a great editor, Ruth Mills, at John Wiley & Sons. To my mind, being a great editor means being a great manager. To pull the best from faltering writers requires a formidable array of personal assets: forbearance and firmness, perseverance and patience, purposiveness and flexibility. Ruth has them all, and I feel privileged to have been able to work with her.

I owe special thanks to Carroll Joynes and Stephen Guittard, both of whom brought their exceptional intelligence and judgment to a scrupulous reading of the manuscript. The book has profited enormously from their suggestions.

I am likewise grateful to others who read portions of the text and made many valuable comments for revision: William Ackman, Marilyn Bane, Wendy Brawer, Christopher Brawer, Nicholas Brawer, Steven Masket, and Abraham Kanner.

In sharing her insights as a writer and her experience as a businesswoman, Randy Rosen was particularly helpful to me when this book was still in its conceptual stage.

A number of friends and acquaintances have stimulated my thinking about the connection between great literature and human issues in management. Daniel Sharp helped me ask myself the right kinds of questions about the ideas I have taken up in these pages. Robert Kavesh and John Flaherty generously shared with me their own experiences teaching literature about the world of commerce to graduate business students. Kevin Brine has been an inspiring example of the humanist as successful executive. George Boynton has proven to me that a background in classical philosophy may be one of the best credentials for the practical business manager. George Newlin shared with me his encyclopedic knowledge of Anthony Trollope's novels about business and businesspeople. Ron Pinciaro, William Peters, Jon Minikes and Susan Backstrom each sharpened my understanding of particular management problems.

I am equally grateful for the thought-provoking conversations I had with the following people who provided valuable perspectives on many issues raised in this book: Carolyn Buck Luce, Robert Brudno, George Wu, David Deutchman, Michael Tischman, Stephen Moses, Irma Zardoya, Ida Kivelevich, Barbara Groves, Nancy Morgan, Frank Guittard, Clare McLean, and Sidney Grant.

Finally, I feel I owe a general debt to all of the people over the past two decades who have shared their own insights on literature in the book discussion groups I have led at the Chappaqua Library, at the Katonah Museum of Art, and at the Lotos Club in New York City.

INDEX

243